M...
Cambridge, Massachusetts

Written by Susie Lee

Edited by Kimberly Moore

Layout by Adam Burns

*Additional contributions by Omid Gohari,
Christina Koshzow, Chris Mason, Joey Rahimi,
and Luke Skurman*

ISBN # 1-4274-0098-9
ISSN # 1551-1133

Last updated 4/22/08

Special Thanks To: Babs Carryer, Andy Hannah, LaunchCyte, Tim O'Brien, Bob Sehlinger, Thomas Emerson, Andrew Skurman, Barbara Skurman, Bert Mann, Dave Lehman, Daniel Fayock, Chris Babyak, The Donald H. Jones Center for Entrepreneurship, Terry Slease, Jerry McGinnis, McGinty, Kyle Russell, Jacque Zaremba, Larry Winderbaum, Roland Allen, Jon Reider, Team Evankovich, Lauren Varacalli, Abu Noaman, Mark Exler, Daniel Steinmeyer, Jared Cohon, Gabriela Oates, David Koegler, and Glen Meakem.

Bounce-Back Team: Kathryn Ann, Jessie Wang, and Austin Neudecker.

College Prowler®
5001 Baum Blvd.
Suite 750
Pittsburgh, PA 15213

Phone: 1-800-290-2682
Fax: 1-800-772-4972
E-Mail: info@collegeprowler.com
Web Site: www.collegeprowler.com

How this all started...

When I was trying to find the perfect college, I used every resource that was available to me. I went online to visit school websites; I talked with my high school guidance counselor; I read book after book; I hired a private counselor. Sure, this was all very helpful, but nothing really told me what life was like at the schools I cared about. These sources weren't giving me enough information to be totally confident in my decision.

In all my research, there were only two ways to get the information I wanted.

The first was to physically visit the campuses and see if things were really how the brochures described them, but this was quite expensive and not always feasible. The second involved a missing ingredient: the students. Actually talking to a few students at those schools gave me a taste of the information that I needed so badly. The problem was that I wanted more but didn't have access to enough people.

In the end, I weighed my options and decided on a school that felt right and had a great academic reputation, but truth be told, the choice was still very much a crapshoot. I had done as much research as any other student, but was I 100 percent positive that I had picked the school of my dreams?

Absolutely not.

My dream in creating *College Prowler* was to build a resource that people can use with confidence. My own college search experience taught me the importance of gaining true insider insight; that's why the majority of this guide is composed of quotes from actual students. After all, shouldn't you hear about a school from the people who know it best?

I hope you enjoy reading this book as much as I've enjoyed putting it together. Tell me what you think when you get a chance. I'd love to hear your college selection stories.

Luke Skurman
CEO and Co-Founder
lukeskurman@collegeprowler.com

Welcome to College Prowler®

During the writing of College Prowler's guidebooks, we felt it was critical that our content was unbiased and unaffiliated with any college or university. We think it's important that our readers get honest information and a realistic impression of the student opinions on any campus—that's why if any aspect of a particular school is terrible, we (unlike a campus brochure) intend to publish it. While we do keep an eye out for the occasional extremist—the cheerleader or the cynic—we take pride in letting the students tell it like it is. We strive to create a book that's as representative as possible of each particular campus. Our books cover both the good and the bad, and whether the survey responses point to recurring trends or a variation in opinion, these sentiments are directly and proportionally expressed through our guides.

College Prowler guidebooks are in the hands of students throughout the entire process of their creation. Because you can't make student-written guides without the students, we have students at each campus who help write, randomly survey their peers, edit, layout, and perform accuracy checks on every book that we publish. From the very beginning, student writers gather the most up-to-date stats, facts, and inside information on their colleges. They fill each section with student quotes and summarize the findings in editorial reviews. In addition, each school receives a collection of letter grades (A through F) that reflect student opinion and help to represent contentment, prominence, or satisfaction for each of our 20 specific categories. Just as in grade school, the higher the mark the more content, more prominent, or more satisfied the students are with the particular category.

Once a book is written, additional students serve as editors and check for accuracy even more extensively. Our bounce-back team—a group of randomly selected students who have no involvement with the project—are asked to read over the material in order to help ensure that the book accurately expresses every aspect of the university and its students. This same process is applied to the 200-plus schools College Prowler currently covers. Each book is the result of endless student contributions, hundreds of pages of research and writing, and countless hours of hard work. All of this has led to the creation of a student information network that stretches across the nation to every school that we cover. It's no easy accomplishment, but it's the reason that our guides are such a great resource.

When reading our books and looking at our grades, keep in mind that every college is different and that the students who make up each school are not uniform—as a result, it is important to assess schools on a case-by-case basis. Because it's impossible to summarize an entire school with a single number or description, each book provides a dialogue, not a decision, that's made up of 20 different topics and hundreds of student quotes. In the end, we hope that this guide will serve as a valuable tool in your college selection process. Enjoy!

OMID GOHARI ◯ CHRISTINA KOSHZOW ◯ CHRIS MASON ◯ JOEY RAHIMI ◯ LUKE SKURMAN ◯
The College Prowler Team

Table of Contents

Introduction from the Author

The Massachusetts Institute of Technology (MIT) is, unquestionably, one of the most respected colleges in the nation, and its alumni are among the most respected in the world. Being that it's the premier school in many science and engineering fields, MIT students have the reputation for being math and science geniuses. Contrary to popular belief, though, MIT is not a place where students spend their free time building mega computers or watching *Star Trek* marathons on Friday nights. True, these people do exist here, but you're more likely to find fellow students who like to lift weights, play basketball, or go club hopping than you are to find Lewis Skolnik clones who program CPUs "just for kicks."

The purpose of this book is to show you some of the other aspects of the school that no one realizes except for the people who go here. From the ins and outs of the dining system, to understanding the different dorms, there are many things that MIT won't tell you in its standard information packets. In fact, there are a lot of things that students don't learn about until they are upperclassmen.

One of the most unique things about MIT is that it is almost impossible to generalize anything about this school. MIT's admissions office chooses people who are exceptional, and these people shape all the different aspects of life on campus. So, forget everything you've heard, and forget all the stereotypes, because MIT is a school that will constantly surprise you, unless, of course, you read this book. Good luck!

Susie Lee, Author
Massachusetts Institute of Technology

By the Numbers

General Information

MIT
77 Massachusetts Avenue
Cambridge, MA 02139

Control:
Private

Academic Calendar:
4-1-4

Religious Affiliation:
None

Founded:
1861

Web Site:
www.mit.edu

Main Phone:
(617) 253-1000

Admissions Phone:
(617) 253-4791

Student Body

**Full-Time
Undergraduates:**
4,068

**Part-Time
Undergraduates:**
59

**Total Male
Undergraduates:**
2,310

**Total Female
Undergraduates:**
1,817

Admissions

Overall Acceptance Rate:
13%

Total Applicants:
11,374

Total Acceptances:
1,514

Freshman Enrollment:
1,002

Yield (% of admitted students who actually enroll):
66%

Early Decision Available?
No

Early Action Available?
Yes

Early Action Deadline:
November 1

Early Action Notification:
December 15

Regular Decision Deadline:
January 1

Regular Decision Notification:
March 20

Must-Reply-By Date:
May 1

Applicants Placed on Waiting List:
389

Applicants Accepting Place on Waiting List:
319

Student Enrolled from Waiting List:
40

Transfer Applications Received:
269

Transfer Applications Accepted:
17

Transfer Students Enrolled:
15

Transfer Applicant Acceptance Rate:
6%

Common Application Accepted?
No

Supplemental Forms?
No

Admissions E-mail:
admissions@mit.edu

Admissions Web Site:
http://web.mit.edu/admissions

SAT I or ACT Required?
SAT required for some

SAT I Range (25th–75th Percentile):
1380–1560

SAT I Verbal Range (25th–75th Percentile):
660–720

**SAT I Math Range
(25th–75th Percentile):**
760–800

SAT II Requirements:
Must take two SAT II tests, one
each in math and science

Retention Rate:
97%

Application Fee:
$65

**Top 10% of High
School Class:**
97%

Financial Information

Full-Time Tuition:
$34,750

Room and Board:
$10,400

Books and Supplies:
$1,114

**Per-Credit-Hour or
Per-Course Charges:**
$545

**Average Need-Based
Financial Aid Package
(including loans, work-study,
grants, and other sources):**
$26,013

**Students Who Applied
for Financial Aid:**
70%

**Applicantts Who Received
Aid:**
80%

Financial Aid Deadline:
February 15

Financial Aid Phone:
(617) 258-8600

Financial Aid E-mail:
ssc@mit.edu

Financial Aid Web Site:
*http://web.mit.edu/sfs/
financial_aid*

Academics

The Lowdown On...
Academics

Degrees Awarded:
Bachelor's
Master's
Doctoral

Most Popular Majors:
36% Engineering
15% Computer Science
11% Physical Sciences
10% Biology/Biological
Sciences
7% Business/Commerce

Undergraduate Schools:
School of Architecture
and Planning
School of Engineering
School of Humanities, Arts,
and Social Sciences
Sloan School of Management
School of Science
Whitaker College of Health
Sciences and Technology

Full-Time Faculty:
1,191

**Faculty with
Terminal Degree:**
92%

**Student-to-Faculty
Ratio:**
7:1

Average Course Load:
48 units (4 classes)

Graduation Rates:
Four-Year: 82%
Five-Year: 91%
Six-Year: 93%

AP Test Score Requirements
Possible credit for scores of 4 or 5

IB Test Score Requirements
Possible credit for scores of 6 or 7

Sample Academic Clubs
American Medical Student Association, Asian Business
Club, Biomedical Engineering Society, BioPharma Business
Club, Finance Club, Management Consulting Club,
Marketing Club, National Society of Black Engineers,
Society of Physics Students

Did You Know?

Eleven current faculty members have been awarded the Nobel Prize in subjects such as physics, physiology of medicine, economics, and chemistry.

Every January, MIT holds its Independent Activities Period (IAP) when **students can stay on campus for four weeks** to take part in activities that are not offered during the regular school year. IAP features workshops, independent research projects, field trips, and lecture series based on subjects ranging from figure skating and vegetarian cooking, to neuroanatomy and robot design.

Adjusting to MIT is a shock. Because of this, MIT gives you a cushion by not assigning first-semester freshmen grades on their transcripts. They simply get a "pass," or the transcript never shows that they took the class. Unless you're in pre-med, no one ever sees your real grades. Freshmen used to be on the Pass/No Record system both semesters, but MIT recently changed the system. Pass/No Record only applies to the first term of freshmen year now. During this time, it's important that you realize right away that **a C- in a class is going to look the same on your transcript as an A+**. What's more, a fair percentage of first-semester students fail at least one class. It's not something to stress about. In other words, don't sweat your work too much first semester. Try to enjoy the city and its people. When you actually start getting graded, you won't have much time to.

Best Places to Study:

Barker Engineering library
Hayden library
Lewis music Library
Reading room

Students Speak Out On...
Academics

{ **"There are two types of classes at MIT: those you participate actively in and those you fall asleep in. I feel like the best classes are the ones where you feel like you can approach the professor anytime."**

Q "Teachers are great. Even as a freshman, **you have lots of resources available** in the form of tutoring, teaching assistants, and upperclassmen."

Q "In general, I've liked most of the teachers that I've had. There are some really great teachers here (both professors and teaching assistants), and there are some really bad ones. One of the important things is to **talk to upperclassmen and ask about what classes and professors are good**."

Q "Teachers are the best in their fields, often having discovered, developed, or decoded the subject they are teaching. **This makes them incredibly knowledgeable, although, not always the best teachers**. Classes and assignments are not very interactive, but they are intensely difficult."

Q "The course instructors vary. While some teachers are very enthusiastic about the topics they teach (for example, **Professor Thomas Allen teaching 15.301**—the Management Psychology Lab—has taught the course for many year's and he still brings such liveliness to the lectures), others seem bored. Upon entering MIT, just ask the upperclassmen for the best instructors, and you can't go wrong."

Q "At MIT, **you will find that professors are very much occupied with research**. There are some who are really good at teaching, and I've built a lot of good, strong relationships over the years. I am impressed with how much they know, but once you get to college, everything's just hard. The big difference in teaching comes in the selection of a smaller school versus a bigger one, and it also depends on whether you'll be doing science or humanities. That's important to know. If you're going to study English, don't come to MIT."

Q "Teachers are a mix of really energetic professors who are truly excited to be teaching us, and those who are old, crusty, and very out of touch with students today. Then there are those who are working on amazing projects, and they are sharing their work with their students, and there are some professors who are so wrapped in their own work and research that **teaching seems to be an afterthought**; they treat students as a second or third priority."

Q "Most of the classes at MIT are taught by professors (with a few exceptions taught by graduate teaching assistants). Teachers run the gamut of being excellent professors who are engaging and accessible, to those who talk only of themselves. However, the quality of a class is not solely determined by the quality of its professor. Teaching assistants and lab assistants can also make the class interesting and enjoyable for you. In my experience, most **professors really do care about feedback** from their students, and they definitely do make active efforts to improve the content of their classes and their various methods of teaching."

Q "Sometimes, you have **foreign TAs that may be a bit hard to understand**, but the professors, for the most part, are really good."

Q "It is hard—don't take that lightly. **At MIT, you'll work your tail off for a C and be proud of it**. People do get As, but I'm just not one of them."

The College Prowler Take On...
Academics

The academics at MIT are top notch. Classes are designed so you learn as much as possible. But learning at MIT doesn't mean just memorizing a formula and plugging in numbers. Exams at MIT are designed to test your knowledge and understanding of the formulas, how to derive them, and how to apply them in all sorts of ways. Classes teach you how to think. However, not all classes are taught well. Some professors are more interested in their research than teaching, and some TAs just don't know how to speak English. Most introductory classes are taught as a combination, of lectures by professors and recitations by TAs. In large classes, however, students are allowed to change their recitations. Take advantage of this! Some TAs explain things better, some are easier graders, some are more available outside of class, and some actually speak understandable English. Try to go to as many different recitations as you can at the beginning of the term to find out which TA suits you best. The extra time you spend looking for a good recitation will save you hours of struggling later in the semester.

Classes are rigorous, but academic opportunities outside the classroom are endless. One of the best academic programs at MIT is the Undergraduate Research Opportunities Program (UROP). As an undergraduate, you have the chance to work for professors who are legendary in their fields. Get involved with a UROP by letting professors know you're interested. Given the studious culture of MIT, expect to do a lot of work. Not all your time, however, will be devoted to classes. You will want to get involved in extracurricular activities and research opportunities. Despite the heavy workload, the things you can accomplish within and beyond the classroom at MIT are miles above anything you could do anywhere else. This is what sets MIT apart as one of the best academic institutions in the country.

The College Prowler® Grade on
Academics: A+

A high Academics grade generally indicates that professors are knowledgeable, accessible, and genuinely interested in their students' welfare. Other determining factors include class size, how well professors communicate, and whether or not classes are engaging.

Local Atmosphere

The Lowdown On...
Local Atmosphere

Region:
Northeast

City, State:
Cambridge, Massachusetts

Setting:
Urban

Distance from New York City:
4 hours

Points of Interest:
Boston Public Library
Boston Symphony Orchestra
Fenway Park
Freedom Trail and related Boston historic sites
Museum of Fine Arts
Public Gardens

Closest Shopping Malls:
Cambridge Galleria
Copley
Newbury Street
Prudential Center

→

Closest
Movie Theaters:

AMC Fenway 13
401 Park Drive Ste. 7
Boston, MA 02215
(617) 424-6266

Copley Theatre
100 Huntington Ave.
Boston, MA 02116
(617) 266-1300

Loews Boston Commons
175 Tremont St.
Boston, MA 02111
(617) 423-3499

Kendall Square Cinema
One Kendall Square
Cambridge, MA 02139
(617) 494-9800

Major Sports Teams:

Bruins (hockey)
Celtics (basketball)
Patriots (football)
Red Sox (baseball)

City Web Sites

www.boston.com will give you all of the info and links
you need to keep up with local news, entertainment, and
restaurant listings. Any Boston information not on the Web site
can probably be easily accessed through one of the links listed
at this site.

www.boston-online.com features its own "wicked hot
Boston topics" and will give you a local feel for the stories the
natives are talking about. It contains plenty of links to what's
happening throughout the city.

Did You Know?

Go to the MIT museum. It is an **interactive, hands-on museum** displaying Artificial Intelligence, Hall of Holograms, Mechanical Artwork, and other really incredible exhibits. Best of all, it is only $2 to get in with your student ID.

5 Fun Facts about Boston:

• There are **"boat-cars" touring the city** at all hours of the day called the Boston Duck Tours. If you make eye contact with the travelers atop this vehicle and shout, "Quack!" they will turn to you and simultaneously reply, "Quack, Quack!"

• A **dead body being dragged out of the Charles River** happens way too often. Do not, repeat, *do not* go swimming on an evening of drunken self-exploration. This is a bad idea. Also avoid contact of said water with both face and other bodily cavities, because the Charles has been polluted for years.

• The **Longfellow Bridge** is the only place in the nation where a plane can fly over a car, traveling over a train, going over a boat (or submarine or hovercraft, etc.).

• **Blue Man Group originated here**. Student rush tickets cost only $25 and can be picked up an hour before the show.

• Kurt Vonnegut wrote the majority of his autobiography, *Slapstick*, set just outside of the **Boston Public Gardens**, where he grew up.

Famous Bostonians:

Aerosmith (all band members)

Ben Affleck

Matt Damon

Conan O'Brien

Mark Wahlberg (the artist formerly known as Marky Mark)

Local Slang:

Drop your R's—they have no business in this city. For way more than you ever wanted to know about Boston slang, visit the *Wicked Good Guide to Boston English* at **www.boston-online.com/glossary.html**.

John Steinbeck's famous novel, *The Grapes of Wrath* (1939) is makes a good point:

"'Everybody says words different,' said Ivy. 'Arkansas folks says 'em different, and Oklahomy folks says 'em different. And we seen a lady from Massachusetts, an' she said 'em different of all. Couldn't hardly make out what she was sayin'!'"

Students Speak Out On...
Local Atmosphere

{ **"Boston rocks! The only downside is that shops close at like 5 p.m. and restaurants at 10 p.m., so there is not that much, besides bars and clubs, to do at night."**

Q "Since the Boston/Cambridge area is filled with colleges (Harvard, Boston University, Boston College, Wellesley, and Tufts). It is a definitely a city with a college atmosphere. **Around MIT, there are great ethnic places to eat**, shopping places, and more. There's nothing that I would say to stay away from except for that little liberal arts college down the street from us (also known as Harvard)."

Q "Boston is **quaint, but not small**—friendly colonial."

Q "Boston has way above the average percentage of residents under 25. It's definitely an **exciting place to go to school**."

Q "You can visit downtown Boston, which has museums, the Symphony Hall (where MIT students get a discount), shopping outlets, and food places. There's a mall within walking distance (there is a shuttle that goes to it from MIT), the MIT museum (which lets in MIT students for free), the Museum of Science (which also lets in MIT students for free), and **basically anything you could ever want**."

Q "Boston is a college city. It is well known for being home to more than 50 colleges and universities within the city and its surrounding suburbs. Harvard is down the street, Boston University is across the river, and many other schools are easily accessible by either bus or subway. **Boston businesses cater to the college crowd** with distinctive shopping areas and restaurants that are upbeat and modern. There are also many museums (Museum of Fine Art, Museum of Science, Harvard Peabody Museum just to name a few), galleries (find them on or around Newbury Street), nightlife venues, and sports arenas to keep you on your toes. With so much to do, so much to see, the atmosphere in Boston is vibrant and colorful."

Q "Boston is probably the best city to be in as a college student. There is so much to do. The shopping is great, and there is no sales tax. **There is a lot of history**, yet at the same time, there are so many colleges nearby that the city doesn't seem old and outdated. As an MIT student, you can get into the Museum of Science, the Museum of Fine Arts, and the MIT museum for free. You should also check out Boston Symphony Orchestra concerts, Blue Man Group, and the Boston Ballet. All of them have student-rush tickets."

Q "MIT is a blend of work and play. It is in the heart of Cambridge/Boston, where a ton of other colleges are present. Throughout the week, **MIT students rarely experience the world outside our campus** due to the workload. However, on most weekends, the fun begins. Students from surrounding colleges like to come to the frat parties. Things to see: the Museum of Science, ice-skating at the Frog Pond in the winter, Walden Pond in the fall (need a car), and Salem, famous for the Salem Witch Trials."

Q "We are in Cambridge. There's something like 60 schools in the Boston area. Harvard and MIT are in Cambridge. We're both along the Charles River. Boston University, Tufts, and Boston College are some other nearby schools. Cape Cod is fun to visit. New York City is also great—it's four hours away by Chinatown bus, and it costs $15. **It's nice and cheap, so we go to New York every now and then**."

The College Prowler Take On...
Local Atmosphere

MIT is located in Cambridge, MA, about a 10-minute walk from Boston. In fact, a large percentage of students actually live in Boston in the various MIT sponsored FSILGs (Fraternities, Sororities, and Independent Living Groups). Boston is the perfect college town. Sandwiched between Harvard and Boston University, MIT is in the hub of the ultimate college city. With so many high-quality schools in the area, Boston is a city that is driven by young, hip, and ambitious students. Because of the thousands of college students wandering the streets, many Boston businesses cater to this population. Concerts, clubs, restaurants, and malls are everywhere. One of the great things about Boston is that all big music names will make a stop here while they're on tour. Also, be sure to check out some of the local bands; they can be incredible.

In addition, public transportation is fairly reliable and convenient. But if you're feeling cheap, you can walk wherever you want to go. Boston is small relative to places like New York City, and walking is an integral part of life here. And every now and then, you may see some famous people walking around or hanging out on Newbury Street and Boylston Street. Don't forget to go see some of the landmarks. Walk the Freedom Trail. Go see a Red Sox game in Fenway Park. Going to college in Boston is an experience unlike any other. Unfortunately, some students at MIT get so wrapped up in their schoolwork that the only problem with living in Boston is finding the time to enjoy it.

The College Prowler® Grade on
Local Atmosphere: A+

A high Local Atmosphere grade indicates that the area surrounding campus is safe and scenic. Other factors include nearby attractions, proximity to other schools, and the town's attitude toward students.

www.collegeprowler.com

Safety & Security

The Lowdown On...
Safety & Security

MIT Police:
55 sworn officers

MIT Police Phone:
Just dial 100 from any
campus phone

Safety Services:
Blue emergency phones
Emergency medical services
Late-night transportation
SafeRide

Health Services:
Provides everything you'd want

(617) 253-1311

Health Center
Office Hours:
The Health Center is open
from 8:30 a.m.–5 p.m.,
Monday through Friday.

Don't worry, emergency
medical care is available 24
hours a day, 7 days a week.

Students Speak Out On...
Safety & Security

"I don't think safety or security is an issue at all here at MIT. I've never even heard of any major issues concerning safety."

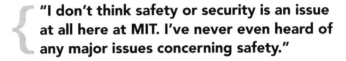

"I feel very safe on campus. **It's Boston though, so you just have to use street smarts** when you're outside campus. Generally, I travel in groups or with other people late at night. The dorms are pretty safe, too. We all exercise open-door policy, and I've never had anything taken from my room."

"MIT's campus is very safe. Despite being surrounded by heavy urban areas, MIT tends to have a fairly isolated feeling, and **a small woman can walk across campus at 4 a.m., half-naked, without feeling unsafe**. There are places to avoid at certain times of day, but they're trivial."

"Campus security is great, though it is rarely needed. On this campus, nothing happens. There has never been a time when I feared for my life or was even too scared to walk to my dorm at 4 a.m. (yes, I was up doing work that late). My female friends say the same thing. They never fear that anything will happen. However, **there are situations at times (burglaries, harassment, rape) but they are few and far between**. If you should ever need campus police, they are always ready to help. There are blue emergency phones all over campus if you ever need one."

Q **"I've always felt perfectly safe since I've been here**. Even when I've ended up coming back from lab at God knows when."

Q **"MIT is in a city and has some problems with theft**, but keeping the door to your room locked usually fixes that. In general, the campus and the area around it is fine, as long as you're careful at night"

Q "I feel completely safe on campus. There are 'blue-light' phones that are always nearby. **Campus police constantly patrol across campus** at night."

Q "MIT has a very safe campus. All the dorms have security at the door. Use your ID cards when entering your dorm, but you must phone the front desk if you wish to visit another dorm. **Some people find it a hassle**, but I like the fact that MIT really takes the safety of its students seriously. At night, there are security guards that patrol the floors of each dorm, and police cruisers make rounds throughout the campus. Emergency telephone booths are also around as an additional safety feature."

Q "For the most part, it is relatively safe on campus. However, it's important that you are always cautious, especially late at night—we do go to school near a large city. **The dorms are pretty safe, but it doesn't hurt to always lock your door**."

Q **"It's fairly safe, but it could be better**. At night, the SafeRide shuttles allow students to get from academic buildings to their residences safely and conveniently."

The College Prowler Take On...
Safety & Security

MIT provides several services in the interest of increasing campus security. First, student IDs are required at every dorm, and your ID only gives you access the dorm you live in. However, security in some dorms is better than in others. Next, MIT runs a shuttle service after 6 p.m. called SafeRide from campus to various student living groups in Boston. Additionally, the campus police provide nighttime transportation for any students who request it. Finally, MIT has installed blue-light emergency phones all over campus that dial up 911 services.

As with any other city, Boston does have its share of safety issues and concerns. Since MIT is fairly self-contained, however, safety isn't a problem on campus. The most common crime on campus is theft, usually of bikes or laptops. If you own a bike, be sure to lock it up. In fact, if you are planning on buying a bike, try not to buy one that's too nice, because it will become a target. During the day, Boston and Cambridge are just about as safe as you can get. And although problems are uncommon even at night, students still need to exercise caution. Walking around the campus late at night is not an issue. However, students should know better than to walk around the city late at night by themselves. If you're going out at night, make sure to have a friend with you.

The College Prowler® Grade on

Safety & Security: B

A high grade in Safety & Security means that students generally feel safe, campus police are visible, blue-light phones and escort services are readily available, and safety precautions are not overly necessary.

Computers

The Lowdown On...
Computers

High-Speed Network?
Yes

Number of Computers:
1,100

Wireless Network?
Yes

Operating Systems:
UNIX-based Athena, Mac, PC

Number of Labs:
19, all 24-hour labs

Free Software

Adobe Reader 7.0, BrioQuery 5.5.6, ESRI, Eudora 5.2.1, Dreamweaver, Host Explorer 6.0.2, iPassConnect 2.40, Maple, Netscape 7.02, Oracle 9i Client Core, VirusScan Enterprise 7.0, WinZephyr 1.1 (beta), and X-Win32 5.4.2, to name a few.

Discounted Software

Abaqus, ESRI, I-DEAS, MAPLE, Mathmatica, Matlab

Charge to Print?

None

Did You Know?

AOL Instant Messenger is based on a program called Zephyr that was created (and is still used) at MIT.

Students Speak Out On...
Computers

"There are computers galore. But if you're coming to MIT, you already have built three of your own, and you have to have one next to your bed so you can check e-mail in your sleep. Right?"

Q "Given that MIT is of the most technologically-advanced schools in the world, its network is usually very quick. At times, when a lot of people are using it, it tends to slow down, but for the most part, you never have to wait. **Computer labs can get crowded, but there are enough of them around campus** so you won't have to wait to use one. I strongly suggest you bring your own computer if you decide to come here. I have found that it makes doing assignments much easier. Although there are computer labs (we call them Athena clusters) in every dorm, there are usually no more than six computers in there, and they can become occupied quite quickly."

Q "**Almost all students have their own personal computers (a mix of desktops and notebooks)**, and although it is possible to get by without one, I don't recommend it. Athena (the campus network operating system) clusters are everywhere, and they are open 24 hours. The network is generally very good and very quick. The campus has about 75 percent coverage with wireless Internet, so having a laptop with a wireless card is definitely an asset."

Q "I've never been unable to find a space in the Athena cluster, but I try to stay away during finals time. **It's a nice way to avoid having to buy a printer**, although the computers are amazingly slow."

Q "There are lots of public labs, and they're only crowded during the middle of the day. The network is generally fine, though the dorm networks are congested. MIT recommends that you bring a computer, though it certainly isn't necessary. I didn't bring one, and I didn't get one until my senior year. **You might wait until you come to see if you really want one** since it doesn't take long if you order from Dell, Gateway, Compaq, or whatever."

Q "You should definitely bring your own computer. There are many computer labs, but I feel like it's more convenient to bring your own computer. **If you are from the West Coast, buy a laptop**! You'll be so happy when it comes to packing your computer for the summer!"

Q "There are lots of Athena clusters all over the place. Most people have their **own computers just because it's really convenient** when you're writing a seven-page paper at 3 a.m., and you don't want to trek all the way to campus."

Q "The Athena computer labs kick butt. They're always open and rarely crowded. **Bringing your own computer is a very, very, good idea**, though."

Q "As a 'tech' school, MIT has computer clusters and computer quick stations all over campus open 24 hours a day. Wireless Ethernet is also installed in many of the dorms and academic buildings. At any hour of the day, you will find students studying, researching, programming, or even sleeping in that spacious computer room. While most students bring their own computers to school, **many often prefer to work at one of the computer clusters for better concentration** or for access to more sophisticated software applications. During exam weeks, these clusters are guaranteed to be crowded, so having your own computer will be convenient then."

The College Prowler Take On...
Computers

Considering MIT's reputation, it should come as no surprise that computers are everywhere on campus. The large number of computer labs (commonly known as "clusters") don't even include the various "quick stations" (one or two computers primarily used for checking e-mail) set up all around campus. The network, known as Athena, was designed in the mid '80s, long before network computing was commonplace. Today, students use public workstations to check e-mail, download music, finish papers, analyze data, and much more. Finding an available workstation is usually very easy, although you should avoid the main clusters the day before large computer science classes have projects due, and also around finals time. In fact, it's always good to know where a few of the smaller clusters are in order to avoid crowds.

Although Athena has everything you could possibly want, you should bring your own computer. The main reason is convenience. MIT students have strange hours and habits, so having your computer allows you to do your work when and how you want. Most of main campus has a reliable wireless network, so it's a good idea to consider buying a laptop. That way, you can work or surf the Web on campus, outside, or even during class. The laptop is also convenient for those students whose homes are far away. Not only can you take all your files with you when you go home for vacations, but you also don't have to worry about hauling your monitor to storage. However, as with all valuables, just make sure you're careful with your computer, as laptop theft does occur now and then.

The College Prowler® Grade on
Computers: A+

A high grade in Computers designates that computer labs are available, the computer network is easily accessible, and the campus' computing technology is up-to-date.

Facilities

The Lowdown On...
Facilities

Student Center:
Sratton Student Center

Athletic Center:
DuPont Gymnasium
Johnson Althetics Center
Zesiger Center

Campus Size:
154 acres

Libraries:
11

Popular Places to Chill:
Fifth floor of the student center
First floor lounge in the
student center
Steps of the student center
when the weather is nice

Movie Theater on Campus?

No, but a group on campus called MIT Lecture Series Committee (LSC) regularly shows movies in 10-250 and 26-100. Go to *http://lsc.mit.edu/schedule/current/index.shtml* for details.

Bar on Campus?

Yes, the Thirsty Ear in Ashdown, the Muddy Charles in Walker Memorial, and the Pub at the Stata Center.

Coffeehouse on Campus?

Yes, one in the student center, one in Building 4, one in Lobby 7, and one in the Stata Center.

Students Speak Out On...
Facilities

> "MIT has had some huge renovations—they improved everything from the fitness center to the lab for computer science. The facilities are good, and the food services are slowly improving."

Q "**The student center has everything you could ever want and more**. It has the MIT store where you can buy school supplies, MIT apparel, items for your dorm room, and books to read leisurely (if you have the time)."

Q "Facilities are a mix of beautiful new buildings and older ones in need of renovation and repair. **The Student Center is a good hang-out and meeting spot**, and the athletic building (the Z-Center) is right next door. The Z-Center is an amazingly beautiful place, and a great place to swim or work out (lockers are at a premium)."

Q "The facilities on campus are great. We now have a total of three athletic centers since we got the Z-Center. It holds **an Olympic-size pool and a huge gym** to work out in."

Q "The Student Center holds **a 24-hour convenience store** that is great for grabbing a late night snack."

Q "Facilities are actually pretty good, and they're **constantly being upgraded**."

Q "The facilities are nice, and **there has been a lot of construction for a new pool** and athletic center, as well as new dorms."

Q "The Z-Center, **the newest athletic center is awesome**. It features two floors of machines and weights, as well as an Olympic-size pool and a diving pool. The Student Center has nice couches, a convenience store, four dining places with a variety of foods, a campus store, a bank, and many rooms where activities are held throughout the year."

Q "In terms of places to study, **the Student Center has a reading room, where almost everyone convenes** for a quiet place to study for midterms and finals. There is also a computer lab. Besides all of that, there are conference rooms where groups often hold meetings."

Q "**The facilities on campus are really nice**. The athletic center is awesome. You can go swimming, or use the machines on the second floor. The Student Center has basically everything you need. There's LaVerde's, a market, as well as a dry cleaners, a barbershop, a post office, and a bank."

Q "The Student Center is where we go for late-night snacks, to meet up with friends for lunch or after classes, or to watch a band performance on the front steps. MIT is **constantly trying to bring in new tastes** to spice up the dining options at Stratton Student Center."

The College Prowler Take On...
Facilities

The highlight of MIT facilities is the gorgeous new athletic facility, the Zesiger Center. Opened in 2002, the Z-Center features two pools, six squash courts, an indoor track, and multi-activity courts for basketball, volleyball, and other IMs. Students have access to this state-of-the-art facility free of charge. Moreover, students also have access to personal trainers and certain other services at a premium. The other main student facility is the Stratton Student Center. The first floor was refurnished with comfortable couches, tables, and additional seating. The various shops and restaurants inside are constantly changing. The student center includes a large reading room, a small market, a post office, a barbershop, a dry cleaner's, an arcade, and a copy shop. The highlight of the Student Center, however, are the many available lounges and meeting areas for students. Because dorms and living groups are so spread out, students often choose to meet in the Student Center to eat, work, and socialize.

As far as other facilities on campus are concerned, MIT is constantly trying to improve. With the opening of the Z-Center, the only complaint that students have is the often eccentric architecture of the buildings. But at a unique place like MIT, the distinctive buildings do fit in nicely. Overall, most facilities on campus offer students their own preferred places to hang out, study, and make themselves comfortable.

B+

The College Prowler® Grade on
Facilities: B+

A high Facilities grade indicates that the campus is aesthetically pleasing and well-maintained; facilities are state-of-the-art, and libraries are exceptional. Other determining factors include the quality of both athletic and student centers and an abundance of things to do on campus.

Campus Dining

The Lowdown On...
Campus Dining

Freshman Meal Plan Requirement?

Minimums depend on which dorm you live in. Dorms with dining halls include a meal plan charge of about $200. Students who pay this get discounted meals in the dorm dining halls.

Meal Plan Average Cost:

$200–$1400 per semester, pay-as-you-go
($200=2 meals per week, $1400=14 meals per week)

Places to Grab a Bite with Your Meal Plan:

Alpine Bagels & Cambridge Grill

Food: Bagels, burgers, pizza, salads, and smoothies

Location: 1st floor Stratton Student Center

Hours: Monday–Thursday 7 a.m.–11 p.m., Friday 7 a.m.–12 p.m., Saturday 9 a.m.–11 p.m., Sunday 9 a.m.–11 p.m.

Anna's Taqueria

Food: Mexican, fried food

Location: 1st floor Stratton Student Center

Hours: Monday–Saturday 7 a.m.–12 a.m., Sunday 8 a.m.–10 p.m.

Baker Dining

Food: Cafeteria-style

Location: Baker House ground floor

Hours: Daily 5 p.m.–8 p.m.

Bio Cafè

Food: Subs, smoothies

Location: Biology building 1st floor

Hours: Monday–Friday 8 a.m–3 p.m.

Bosworth's

Food: Coffee, tea, pastries

Location: Rogers Building

Hours: Monday–Thursday 8 a.m.–6 p.m., Friday 8 a.m.–5 p.m.

Building 4 Cafè

Food: Soup, coffee

Location: Building 4, 1st floor

Hours: Monday–Thursday 8 a.m.–3 p.m., Friday 3:15 p.m.–9 p.m., Saturday–Sunday Closed

Forbes Family Cafè

Food: American, coffee

Location: Building 32

Hours: Monday–Friday 11 a.m.–3 p.m.

LaVerde's Market

Food: Grocery, ready-made hot meals, subs, sandwiches, soup

Location: 1st floor Stratton Student Center

Hours: Monday-Saturday 7 a.m.–12 a.m., Sunday 8 a.m.–10 p.m.

Lobdell Food Court

Food: Burger King, pizza, Mexican, deli, Asian, hometown food

Location: 2nd floor Stratton Student Center

Hours: Monday-Friday 11 a.m.–3 p.m.

McCormick Dining

Food: "Healthy" cafeteria-style

Location: McCormick Hall ground floor

Hours: Sunday–Thursday 5 p.m.–8 p.m.

Next House

Food: Grill, vegetarian

Location: Next House

Hours: Sunday–Thursday, 5 p.m.–8 p.m.

Pacific Java

Food: Coffee, tea, pastries

Location: Simmons Nite Cafe

Hours: Sunday–Thursday
9 p.m.–1 a.m.

Pritchett Grill
at Walker

Food: Pasta entrees, salads,
burgers, fries, snacks

Location: 2nd floor
Walker Memorial

Hours: Sunday–Thursday
4 p.m.–9 p.m.

The R and D Pub

Food: Personal pan pizzas,
fruit, sushi, and alcohol

Location: 4th floor Stata Center

Hours: Monday–Friday
4 p.m.–10 p.m.

Refresher Course

Food: Deli-style

Location: Sloan Building

Hours: Monday–Thursday
8 a.m.–5 p.m., Friday 8 a.m.–
3 p.m.

Simmons Dining

Food: Asian, vegetarian

Location: Building W79

Hours: Sunday–Thursday
5 p.m.–8 p.m.

Steam Cafè

Food: Global, ethnic food

Location: Rogers Building

Hours: Monday–Thursday
8 a.m.–6 p.m., Friday 8 a.m.–
5 p.m.

Off-Campus Places to Use Your Meal Plan:

You can pay for Domino's
delivery with your T card.

24-Hour On-Campus Eating?

LaVerde's Market

Other Options:

MacGregor Convenience
in MacGregor is great for
late night snacks. Also,
Massachusetts Avenue truck
vendors serve food during the
day through the wee hours of
the night.

Students Speak Out On...
Campus Dining

> "Campus food is actually pretty good—it has improved a lot in recent years. It's kind of expensive, though. The flexibility of the dining plan is a big plus. Getting lunch at the food trucks is yummy and cheap."

Q "The dining halls aren't too good. There are food trucks that are pretty good (mobile kitchens in trucks). **Lots of people that I know cook for themselves** since many dorms have kitchens, and there is a supermarket nearby."

Q "Alpine Bagels is good, but a bit expensive. **Meals are expensive and not buffet style**. Pritchett dining is good, but selection is limited. At least, they offer some good veggie options."

Q "In terms of food, our Student Center has a bagel shop (which also has a grill), a crepe store, and one of the main dining places on campus. In that cafeteria, students can get **Burger King, pizza, Mexican food, sandwiches, stir-fry, and all types of beverages**. They also have good options for vegetarians if that interests you."

Q "**The campus food isn't great, but it's improved greatly throughout the years**. Alpine Bagels is okay, the subs at Laverde's are good, and you can always go to the food trucks for late-night snacks."

Q "**Food on campus is average and kind of expensive**. Most students have a declining balance on their ID card that they use to purchase food. LaVerde's is good for pretty much whatever you need. It's sort of like a small grocery store with a sub counter and lots of prepackaged meals. The Student Center also has a bagel café and a full dining hall that is open only for lunch. Other restaurants in the student center are open to 11 or 12 at night."

Q "**It's horrible**. But the dorms all have kitchens, and the off-campus and delivery food is decent—some of it is even pretty cheap."

Q "MIT dining is rather odd, I think. **There's no one big dining hall; there are bunches of smaller eating places**. Lobdell is okay, but I think their food could use a bit more variety."

Q "**It's pretty poor, or so goes the popular sentiment**."

Q "So maybe campus dining isn't MIT's best quality, but the food here is actually pretty decent; the options are getting better. Pritchett and Simmons have the best selection and taste in my opinion. There is also a bagel place that just opened last year, which has a variety of smoothies on its health-conscious menu."

The College Prowler Take On...
Campus Dining

One of the best things about MIT dining is that there are no required "meals" that you have to buy. Instead, *you* decide how much money to credit to your student ID. Then you can spend the money however you like on campus. In addition to the typical dining halls (Lobdell and Walker), MIT also has Alpine Bagels. You can also use your card at the market in the student center, LaVerde's. Although prices tend to be expensive, students should always be able to find something to eat. Most freshmen don't catch on to one of the best lunch deals, the food trucks. There are two food trucks at 77 Mass. Ave., and a large group of them next to the bio building. Not only do the food trucks serve yummy hot food (from pizza, to Chinese, to Mexican), the prices are also unbelievably cheap. For $3.95, you can get a complete Chinese meal at the Chinese food truck.

The most common complaints that students have is the lack of food selection at the regular dining halls. Because various dining halls are only open for lunch or dinner, your options at any given time can vary. Food ranges from hot entrées to cold à la carte items, and vegetarian options are always available. Learn the operating hours of the dining halls—there's nothing more disappointing than walking to the Student Center for a crepe only to find that the restaurant is closed. Laverde's is open 24 hours a day on weekends and open late on weekdays, so satiating late-night munchies won't be a problem. MIT campus dining isn't perfect, but it's improving. One of the main reasons is the friendly and helpful staff. If you have any comments or suggestions, you should let them know because they actually care what you think. Students can suggest meals or even comment on prices, and usually the staff will do what they can to help.

The College Prowler® Grade on
Campus Dining: C+

Our grade on Campus Dining addresses the quality of both school-owned dining halls and independent on-campus restaurants as well as the price, availability, and variety of food.

Off-Campus Dining

The Lowdown On...

Off-Campus Dining

Restaurant Prowler:
Popular Places to Eat!

Ankara Café
Food: Italian, deli sandwiches
472 Commonwealth Ave.
(617) 437-0404
www.ankaracafe.com
Cool Features: Inexpensive, bang for the buck
Prices: $10–$15
Hours: Daily 11:30 a.m.–12 a.m.

Charley's Eating & Drinking Saloon
Food: American, Caribbean
284 Newbury St.
(617) 266-3000
www.dwlz.com/Restaurants/charleysaloon.html
Cool Features: Good fish, some drink specials
Price: $12–$18
Hours: Monday–Thursday 11:30 a.m.–11 p.m., Friday–Saturday 11:30 a.m.–12 a.m., Sunday 11 a.m.–11 p.m.

➜

The Cheesecake Factory

Food: American

100 Cambridgeside Pl.

(617) 252-3810

www.cheesecakefactory.com

Cool Features: Great atmosphere, over 200 menu items

Prices: $9–$21

Hours: Monday–Thursday 11:30 a.m.–11p.m., Friday–Saturday 11:30 a.m.–12:30 p.m., Sunday 10 a.m.–10 p.m. (brunch served until 2:30 p.m.)

Cinderella's

Food: Pizza, Italian

901 Main Street

(617) 576-0280

Cool Features: Open late

Prices: $8–$15

Hours: Monday–Wednesday 11 a.m.–1 a.m., Thursday–Saturday 11 a.m.–2 a.m., Sunday 11 a.m.–1 a.m.

Finale

Food: Dessert, coffee

1 Columbus Ave.

(617) 423-3184

Price: $8–$14

Cool Features: Lipstick-red banquettes and black furniture

Hours: Monday 11:30 a.m.–10:30 p.m., Tuesday–Wednesday 11:30 a.m.–11:30 p.m., Thursday–Friday 11:30 a.m.–12 a.m., Saturday 6 p.m.–12 a.m., Sunday 4 p.m.–11 p.m.

IHOP

Food: Breakfast

1850 Soldiers Field Rd.

(617) 787-0533

www.ihop.com

Cool Features: Stuffed French toast, pancakes galore

Prices: $5–$10

Hours: Daily 24 hours

Island Hopper

Food: Asian

91 Massachusetts Ave.

(617) 266-1618

Price: $8-$20

Cool Features: Child-friendly

Hours: Sunday–Thursday 11:30 a.m.–11 p.m., Friday–Saturday 11:30 a.m.–12 a.m.

Mary Chung's

Food: Chinese

464 Massachusetts Ave.

(617) 864-1991

Cool Features: Cheap, convenient, good service

Price: $5–$10

Hours: Daily 11 a.m.–10 p.m.

Pho Pasteur

Food: Vietnamese

36 JFK St.

(617) 864-4100

Cool Features: Soft lighting, multi-level dining area

Prices: $15–$25

Hours: Daily 11:30 a.m.–10:30 p.m.

The Pour House Bar and Grill

Food: American

909 Boylston St.

(617) 236-1767

www.pourhouseboston.com

Cool Features: Relaxed
restaurant by day, rowdy bar
by night

Price: $10–$18

Hours: Daily 8 a.m.–2 a.m.

Vinny Testa's

Food: Italian, American

867 Boylston St

(617) 262-6699

www.vinnytsofboston.com

Cool Features: Great nocci

Price: $7–$15

Hours: Monday–Thursday
11:30 a.m.–11 p.m. Friday–
Saturday 11:30 a.m.–12 a.m.,
Sunday 12 p.m.–10 p.m.

Late-Night, Half-Price Food Specials:

The Pour House –
Half-off burgers on Saturday
Half-off chicken on Tuesday
Half-off Mexican on Thursday

24-Hour Eating:
IHOP

Closest Grocery Stores:

Haymarket
Blackstone Street

LaVerde's Market
The Student Center

Star Market
26 Sidney Street
Central Square
(617) 494-5250

Student Favorites:
The Cheesecake Factory
Mary Chung's
The Pour House

Best Breakfast:
IHOP

Best Chinese:
Mary Chung's

Best Desserts:
Finale

Best Pizza:
Cinderella's

Best Wings:
The Pour House

Best Place to Take Your Parents:
Charley's Eating &
Drinking Saloon

Other Places to Check Out:
Crazy Dough's (Pizza)
Domino's (Pizza)
Hi-Fi (American)
IHOP (Breakfast)
Larry Burdick's (Chocolate)
The Middle East
(Middle Eastern)
Quan's Kitchen (Chinese)
Thailand Café (Thai)
Union Oyster House
(Seafood, Fine Dining)

Students Speak Out On...
Off-Campus Dining

"There are endless options for places to eat in Boston and Cambridge. Check out Harvard Square and Newbury Street— you'll be sure to find something."

Q "It's Boston. **The quality varies, but quantity never fails**. Pho Pasteur in Harvard Square is terrific and cheap if you like Vietnamese. Mary Chung's Chinese in Central Square (three blocks north of MIT) is a popular place—order the Peking ravioli. There are several good Mexican places if you don't have friends who are allergic, and there are dozens of nice places that you can take your parents to."

Q "There are some good spots for outside food. The Chinese ones include Mary Chung's and Quan's Kitchen. The good Italian places are Cinderella's and Vinny Testa's. **Domino's and Hi-Fi are good for American**."

Q "**There are so many restaurants that you'll never eat at them all**. I recommend Chinatown, the Middle East, and Mary Chung's. There aren't a lot of diners, but IHOP isn't far if you can get a ride."

Q "Close by, there isn't much. **Go into Boston, there's much more**."

Q "There are **lots of restaurants of all kinds near campus**. There is pizza, Chinese, Italian, Indian, and more. There are plenty of cheap places that are good for normal occasions and a couple of nicer places, as well."

Q "Pour House is on Boylston street in Boston, and it's relatively close to campus. Saturdays is half-off burgers night, and you can get a meal for about $3. Thursdays is half-off Mexican food. Charley's is an upscale prime-rib place on Newbury Street. They have the best warm apple crisp. **Larry Burdick's, an adorable chocolate store, is in Harvard Square**, and they make the best hot chocolate. Finale is a dessert restaurant where the food looks like art. There is one in Harvard Square and one in the Theater District. If you want to buy your own fruits and vegetables, go to the Haymarket by Quincy Market. You can get them really cheap, and it's a fun outdoor market."

Q "**There are tons of great restaurants close to campus**. The closest ones (that deliver!) include Thailand Café, Ankara's (deli style), and Cinderella's (authentic Italian). Harvard Square is also just a few T stops away with a great pizza place, Crazy Dough's, and Pho Pasteur, an awesome Vietnamese restaurant. Boston is also right across the bridge with cute restaurants on Newbury where you can shop and eat at the same time."

Q "**Restaurants are great in Boston and Cambridge**. There are tons of places, and there is a lot of variety. Both Vinny Testas and the Pour House are great. It's all good."

Q "There are a lot of good restaurants in Boston and in Harvard Square. **I go into Boston more often**, but there's a lot of good places within walking distance such as the Pour House, Vinny Testas, and the Cheesecake Factory."

The College Prowler Take On...
Off-Campus Dining

No matter what you want to eat, you can find it in Boston. Restaurants range from cheap fast food joints to expensive fine dining. If you're working on a tight budget, you don't need to eat at fast food restaurants every time you eat out. Some restaurants, such as the Pour House on Boylston, have specials on certain nights that make meals less than $5 per person.

Another great thing about off-campus dining in Boston and Cambridge is the variety of ethnic foods that you can find. From authentic Italian dining and historic restaurants, such as the Union Oyster House in the North End, to Mary Chung's in Chinatown, you can find anything you're craving. You can also try something new that you've never eaten before. Given all the hard work that students do during the week, going out on the weekends is a fun break. And because of the erratic hours of campus dining, going out can be the most convenient. If you don't want to go out to eat, a lot of restaurants have delivery services. For example, Thailand Café on Massachusetts Avenue offers cheap meals and fast delivery. Be sure to check the menus, though; some restaurants have minimums for delivery, and others charge a delivery fee. And remember that almost everything in Boston shuts down at 2 a.m. So, if you're hungry during late night, you're out of luck.

The College Prowler® Grade on

Off-Campus Dining: A

A high Off-Campus Dining grade implies that off-campus restaurants are affordable, accessible, and worth visiting. Other factors include the variety of cuisine and the availability of alternative options (vegetarian, vegan, Kosher, etc.).

Campus Housing

The Lowdown On...
Campus Housing

Room Types:
Singles, doubles,
triples, quads

Best Dorms:
New House
MacGregor

Worst Dorms:
Random Hall

**Undergrads Living
on Campus:**
91%

Number of Dorms:
10

**Number of University-
Owned Apartments:**
7

Dormitories:

Baker

Floors: 6

Total Occupancy: 318

Bathrooms: Single and multiple occupancy

Coed: Yes

Room Types: Doubles, Triples, Quads (Singles for upperclassmen only)

Health/Allergy Considerations: Elevators, no smoking, no cats, no carpets.

Special Features: This wave-shaped building, which maximizes the number of rooms with sunny southern exposure and orients them at oblique angles to soften noise from Memorial Drive, is considered a masterpiece.

Bexley

Floors: 4

Total Occupancy: 120

Bathrooms: Communal

Coed: Yes

Room Types: Singles, Suite-style Doubles

Room Types for Freshmen: Doubles

Health/Allergy Considerations: Smoking in certain suites, cats allowed, no carpets.

Special Features: Students are allowed to paint on the soundproof walls of their dorm rooms. Is also home to a Kitchen Chemistry course where students prepare and eat food while learning about the chemistry of cooking.

Burton Connor House

Floors: 10

Total Occupancy: 344

Bathrooms: Multiple occupancy, coed bathrooms, shared with other suite residents

Coed: Yes, although some suites are single sex

Room Types: Singles, Doubles, Triples, Suite-style

Room Types for Freshmen: Doubles, Triples

Health/Allergy Considerations: Elevator, no smoking in common areas, no cats, rooms are carpeted.

Special Features: Burton Conner House has laundry facilities, kitchens by suite or floor, and a weight room.

East Campus

Floors: 5

Total Occupancy: 362

Bathrooms: Several coed bathrooms are shared by hall.

Coed: Yes

Room Types: Singles, Doubles

Room Types for Freshmen: Singles, Doubles

Health/Allergy Considerations: No carpets, two smoking halls, cats allowed.

Special Features: The two buildings of East Campus are connected by an underground tunnel. Each of the 10 halls have their own graduate tutors, and all students share the dorm's own weight room.

MacGregor

Floors: 15

Total Occupancy: 326

Bathrooms: Shared by suite, coed or single-sex, depending on your suite

Coed: Yes

Room Types: Singles

Freshmen Room Types: Singles, Doubles

Health/Allergy Considerations: Elevator, carpets in rooms, no smoking, no cats.

Special Features: MacGregor is set up as a group of "entries." Each entry consists of several suites. Also, MacGregor has it own convenience store.

McCormick Hall

Floors: 7

Total Occupancy: 238

Bathrooms: Two communal bathrooms are shared by each floor

Coed: No, all female

Room Types: Singles, Doubles, Triples

Freshmen Room Types: Doubles, Triples, Singles

Health/Allergy Considerations: Elevators, some rooms carpeted, no smoking, no cats.

Special Features: McCormick is one of the dorms that does Residence Based Advising (RBA). In order to live in McCormick, you have to apply over the summer.

New House

Floors: 5

Total Occupancy: 291

Bathrooms: Coed, communal by floor

Coed: Yes

Room Types: Singles, Doubles, Triples

Freshmen Room Types: Doubles, Triples

Health/Allergy Considerations: No carpeting, no smoking, no cats.

Special Features: There are several cultural groups (Chocolate City, French, Russian, and Spanish) that are all in New House. Also, being one of the newer dorms, New House has air conditioning!

Next House

Floors: 5

Total Occupancy: 347

Bathroom: Several coed bathrooms per floor

Coed: Yes

Room Types: Singles, Doubles, Triples

Freshmen Room Types: Doubles, Triples

Health/Allergy Considerations: Elevators, no carpeting, no smoking, no cats.

Special Features: Next House is also one of the dorms that does RBA. That means you have to apply over the summer.

Random Hall

Floors: 4

Total Occupancy: 93

Bathroom: two private bathrooms per floor

Coed: Yes

Room Types: Doubles

Freshmen Room Types: Doubles

Health/Allergy Considerations: Carpeting, smoking allowed, cats allowed.

Special Features: Each floor is divided into two floor units, each with 3–14 students. Random Hall is the only undergraduate dorm located on the North side of campus. It is also the smallest, and has a computer to human ratio of 3:1.

Senior House

Floor: 4

Total Occupancy: 146

Bathrooms: Coed, communal by floor

Coed: Yes

Room Types: Singles, Doubles

Freshmen Room Types: Doubles

Health/Allergy Considerations: Air conditioning, carpeting, smoking allowed in some halls and suites, cats allowed.

Special Features: The oldest dorm on campus, Senior House is located next to the president's house.

Simmons Hall

Floors: 10

Total Occupancy: 344

Bathrooms: Coed, communal by floor

Coed: Yes

Room Types: Singles, Doubles

Freshmen Room Types: Singles, Doubles

Health/Allergy Considerations: Elevator, no smoking, no cats.

Special Features: MIT's newest undergraduate dorm that seems to have been modeled after a sponge.

Bed Type
Extra-long

Cleaning Service?
Some dorms have housekeeping for public spaces.

What You Get
All dorms have Athena stations, study areas, lounges, computer quick stations, laundry facilities, kitchen, and weight, game, music, and TV rooms.

Did You Know?

Dorms at MIT are run by a House Manager and two faculty Housemasters, usually a married couple. They live right in the dorm along with students offering advice, guiding students through their transitions, and planning fun social activities for residents.

Students Speak Out On...
Campus Housing

"Dorms are alright. If you're not a freak, avoid Senior House—anyone can live there, it's not just for seniors. Random Hall is a little sketchy and far from center campus. Baker and Next are the social dorms."

Q "**Each dorm holds a personality of its own**, so it's to each student's individual taste. While some dorms are older and perhaps more run-down, they may be more convenient. The nice dorms (by my tastes) are: Simmons, McCormick, Baker, and Bexley."

Q "**Each dorm at MIT has a unique personality**. Incoming freshmen get to choose which dorm they want to live in after orientation. Some dorms, like Burton Connor, are a little run-down and may appear cramped. New House and Next House are better furnished, though located farther from classes than most other dorms. Simmons is spacious. Baker House, known as the most social dorm on campus is a long brick building that hosts many barbecues, floor/lounge parties, and roof deck excursions."

Q "The all-female dorm, McCormick, is **nice for those girls who want their own space**. East Campus is famous for its eclectic mix of residents, who often choose to paint and decorate their rooms in funky fashion. Senior House and Random House are a bit apprehensive to outsiders, but they look like interesting places to live."

Q "Depending on your personality, I don't know which dorm to recommend or to tell you to stay away from. Usually, people stay away from East Campus, Senior House, Bexley Hall, and Random Hall. It's not to say that these are bad places to live—some of them have the biggest rooms—but **a lot of the people usually stereotype them as the geek dorms**. That's where the stereotypical MIT student lives. I, personally, live in the new dorm, Simmons Hall. I love it. It's so different from any dorm I have ever seen. Each dorm has something to offer."

Q "**It depends what kind of person you are**. McCormick is all women, very clean, quiet, and kind of boring. Baker is very social, pretty new, kind of loud, and party-ish. Burton Conner has suites, and it's social; people cook here. MacGregor has all singles, and sometimes it's considered antisocial; it depends on what entry you live on. There are also ethnic houses like the French house, Russian house, and German house. Next House has great community spirit, and is a relatively new dorm."

Q "**Simmons is a new dorm**, so its culture is not yet defined. East Campus has lots of drugs, is eccentric, and the rooms are really big. Senior House also has lots of drugs and is eccentric; it was recently renovated."

Q "I really liked the dorm that I lived in (East Campus). **There's some time when you get here to go visit the dorms and meet people there**. You should definitely do that before you decide where to live."

Q "It's okay for a while. **But off-campus (FSILG) housing is way better**."

Q "If you come to MIT, you'd better learn to like the housing on campus. It will cost you an arm and a leg to move off. I've seen many students attempt to live off campus, only to find out that having a job and taking full-time undergrad courses at the same time is not such a good idea—the time constraints for both can be difficult to handle, even for the smartest, most dedicated students. So **do yourself a favor and learn to like, or at least tolerate, your dorm**."

Q "It depends on what you want in a dorm (noise level, number of roommates, kitchens, distance from academic buildings, etc.). In terms of social-ness, for example, Baker is the most social, Next isn't far behind, and Burton Conner and Simmons are not quite as social. **MacGregor and McCormick are pretty quiet**."

The College Prowler Take On...
Campus Housing

The dorms at MIT are as varied as the students. Each dorm has its own culture and reputation. Don't go on stereotypes alone. It's best to ask some current students for their opinions. However, MIT housing has changed in the past year due to freshmen being required to live on campus. Therefore, upperclassmen may not always be the most informed.

MIT is unique in that you get two chances to choose where you live. The summer before your freshman year, you make a choice of dorms. But you also get another chance to choose which dorm you want to live in when you get on campus. There is a period at the end of orientation where dorms will have their "rush." Be careful when you make your choices over the summer. Your decision and dorm assignment could be permanent, for a while at least. After dorm rush, if you think you want to switch dorms, you can put yourself on a waiting list. If you think you want to switch into Baker, put yourself on the list right away. Waiting periods for this dorm can be years. When you make your decision, put some thought into it. If you're still not in your ideal place, don't worry too much because moving is fairly easy. One thing to watch out for, though, is overcrowding. In the past years, Simmons, the newest undergraduate residence, alleviated most of the problems of overcrowding. However, the percentage of undergraduates living on campus has increased greatly due to freshmen housing requirements. Therefore, expect this problem to continue over the next few years.

B-

The College Prowler® Grade on
Campus Housing: B-

A high Campus Housing grade indicates that dorms are clean, well-maintained, and spacious. Other determining factors include variety of dorms, proximity to classes, and social atmosphere.

Off-Campus Housing

The Lowdown On...
Off-Campus Housing

Undergrads in Off-Campus Housing:
9%

Average Rent For:
Studio Apt.: $1,082
1BR Apt.: $1,394
2BR Apt.: $1,758
3BR Apt.: $2,172

For Assistance Contact:
Off-Campus Housing Service
(617) 253-1493
http://web.mit.edu/housing/ och/index.html
eleonore@mit.edu

Note

Rents vary by location and number of rooms. For additional areas around MIT, check out at *http://web.mit. edu/housing/och/rents.html*. You can also check out *www. bostonapartments.com* for help finding an apartment.

Did You Know?

Best Time to Look for a Place

The best time to look for a September rental is in mid to late July.

The best time to look for a January rental is late November and early December.

The best time to look for a summer rental is April and early May.

Students Speak Out On...
Off-Campus Housing

"Most undergrads live on campus because off-campus housing is just not convenient in terms of affordability and location."

Q "FSILG **off-campus housing is way better** than on-campus dorm housing."

Q "Almost all undergraduates live on campus all four years. Frats house brothers, and some sorority sisters have housing, but very few people actually move into apartments as an undergraduate. Independent housing is expensive in the area, and transportation is a hassle if you don't have a car. Plus, **most people stay on campus so they can take advantage of all that MIT has to offer**."

Q "If it isn't in a fraternity or sorority, **avoid off-campus housing like the plague until you're very, very rich**. Cambridge is more expensive than Manhattan."

Q "It is expensive. **People don't generally live off campus in Boston all that much**. Typical housing is $800 or more per month, and that's a really good price, too."

Q "**You don't want to live off campus**. The dorms are great, and if you can find one bedroom to rent in a shared apartment in Cambridge for less than $600 month, you're a miracle worker."

Q "Housing off campus is usually in a Greek house. Other than that, **good luck finding a decent apartment** that's cheap, or even affordable."

The College Prowler Take On...
Off-Campus Housing

For MIT students, off-campus housing means not living in a dorm or FSILG (Fraternities, Sororities, and Independent Living Groups). Although FSILGs aren't exactly on-campus housing, they are affiliated with MIT. Most of their houses are in Boston. And although only seven percent of MIT students live in what we would consider true off-campus housing, a good percent of students (mostly men) live in FSILGs. They provide a relatively inexpensive and well-located alternative to on-campus housing. For more information, check the section on fraternities and sororities.

True off-campus housing means living in an apartment or house that is not affiliated with MIT. And the bottom line is: don't do it. Not only is rent expensive, but actually finding an apartment is a hassle. Off-campus housing also means you will be farther away from your classes and almost all your friends. Do yourself a favor: save the "I want my own apartment" phase until after graduation.

D-

The College Prowler® Grade on
Off-Campus Housing: D-

A high grade in Off-Campus Housing indicates that apartments are of high quality, close to campus, affordable, and easy to secure.

Diversity

The Lowdown On...
Diversity

Native American:
1%

White:
37%

Asian American:
26%

International:
8%

Hispanic:
11%

Unknown:
10%

African American:
6%

Out-of-State:
90%

Students Speak Out On...
Diversity

"Personally, I think the campus is very diverse. I know that is one thing the admissions office strives for. I am a black student at MIT, and I have to say that I am impressed."

Q "As far as diversity is concerned, **it's probably as diverse, or more so, than most other schools**."

Q "Campus is **very diverse**."

Q "**MIT is very ethnically diverse**, but it doesn't mix well. You'll find this problem at any college campus. MIT generates high diversity in international population and ethnic races. There are lots of Asians; sometimes it feels like 70 percent of people here are Asian because I think all the white kids live across the river in frats. Plus, we pick where we live when we get here, so people automatically feel more comfortable with their same race."

Q "It's really diverse. **If you're white and want to see what it's like to be a minority for once, this is the place to experience it**. Well, at least on the East Coast. The diversity isn't just racial; it extends to personalities, beliefs, religions, and so on."

Q "I guess it's **pretty diverse**; I haven't noticed really."

Q "There are lots of different ethnicities and viewpoints on campus. It's great because **everyone can find somewhere they belong**."

Q "MIT is one giant melting pot. Of all the colleges I have visited, MIT is definitely the most diverse. With kids from all 50 states and dozens of countries worldwide, you will see people of all sorts on campus. Although MIT's campus is extremely diverse, **it is also a fact that some students do tend to self-segregate**. I think it is most likely because most people try to stick to what they are familiar with in a place where they are new to. Also, there is no racial tension on campus."

Q "MIT draws in students from very different parts of the world. **The student body is quite diverse economically, socially, and ethnically**."

The College Prowler Take On...
Diversity

The MIT admissions office strives to find brilliant and unique students. On paper, MIT is one of the most diverse campuses in the nation. And this diversity extends well beyond race to religion, background, political viewpoints, and personal beliefs. There are student groups and clubs for every possible interest, including political groups, cultural groups, religious groups, and a variety of combinations in between. The point is that although no two students at MIT are exactly alike, people still want to bond over the things that they share in common.

Racially, the only problem with all the diversity is a slight tendency for self-segregation. Students mingle together in classes and activities, but some living groups and social networks tend to be divided along racial lines. For the most part however, this segregation isn't intentional, and barriers are easily broken. If you have any problems with any races, religions, or beliefs, MIT could shock or maybe even upset you. If you welcome diversity, new experiences, and open exchange of ideas and beliefs, you will be very comfortable here at MIT.

The College Prowler® Grade on
Diversity: A

A high grade in Diversity indicates that ethnic minorities and international students have a notable presence on campus and that students of different economic backgrounds, religious beliefs, and sexual preferences are well-represented.

Guys & Girls

The Lowdown On...
Guys & Girls

Men Undergrads:	Women Undergrads:
56%	44%

Birth Control Available?

Yes. There are free condoms at the Health Center.

Dress Code

The truth is, after the first round of midterms, nobody at MIT has the time or energy to make themselves look great everyday. So don't worry too much about what you should or shouldn't be wearing. Besides, MIT has so many different kinds of people that, no matter what you wear, you won't look weird. Trust me.

Hookups or Relationships?

Both occur at MIT. It just depends on what you're looking for. Since many students are busy with heavy work loads and research projects, there doesn't seem to be much time for committed relationships. Weekend hookups and flirting at the bars is the best option. However, it's not uncommon to find some sweethearts who found love amidst the studying and reading.

Best Places to Meet Guys/Girls

Because most MIT students spend the majority of their time with their noses buried in books, the library is a great place to find someone and strike up a conversation. Most students are friendly and would be happy to take a break and talk with you; they might just need a little encouragement. Classes and extracurricular clubs are also prime spots for finding potential dates or hookups.

Did You Know?

Top Places to Find Hotties:

1. Frat Parties
2. Activities
3. Wellesley College

Students Speak Out On...
Guys & Girls

> **"MIT is definitely underrated in terms of the aesthetics of its populace. Like anywhere else, there are 'hot' people. If you're having problems, there are schools all over the Boston area. Or you can drink."**

Q "Wellesley has a saying about MIT men that I find true: **'MIT men—the odds are good, but the goods are odd.'** There's also a saying about Boston women: 'Wellesley to wed, Simmons to bed, MIT to talk to.' Any other school will have better-looking people than MIT, overall. However, I think all my friends are pretty good-looking people."

Q "There's **always a crowd you can fit in with**."

Q "**Like any college, you get a range of personalities**. You got the crack-heads, drunks, geeks, jocks, and others. You get the point."

Q "There're all kinds here—hot, not, geek, preppy, whatever. They're all intelligent, though. **If you're into geeky guys** who think that handmade, electronic teddy bears and hand-painted war-game miniatures are romantic, this is definitely a good place to start. But, there're plenty of more normal guys and girls out there, and many are interested in playing the field if you're into that sort of thing, too."

Q "The MIT dating scene is entirely a matter of personal opinion. **But sure, I'd say everyone is alright**."

Q "As far as the people go, there's the whole social spectrum here. Take the top three percent or so from all over the world, make it a given that all your peers are smart (a lot of them smarter than you), and just **redistribute the 'scene' from high school**—you've got the nerds, the jocks, and the cool kids. There's anything and everything here, not to mention cultures from all over the planet."

Q "It's way too varied. Remember beauty truly lies within. I've met the most 'beautiful' people at MIT and **I wouldn't have if I was simply concerned with hotness**."

Q "The guys are great. It doesn't seem like there are many hotties, though. And those who are hotties are so arrogant that they aren't hot anymore. But they are very friendly and great guys. However, many guys are in frats, so if you are not used to knocking on frat doors, it may be initially difficult to get to know them. **One thing that I recommend is not jumping into a relationship too early freshman year**. It's more important to establish your close friends first."

Q "MIT is apparently pretty ugly compared to other colleges. **I don't seem to notice** anymore, though."

Q "All in all, the people at MIT are not the most attractive ones in town. That's a fact. However, **you will find your share of funny, intelligent, out-going, and caring people on campus**. If you want a date, there's always Harvard, BU, and so on."

Q "Girls are not hot at all here. **If you are a hot girl, please enroll here**."

The College Prowler Take On...
Guys & Girls

In terms of pure physical attractiveness, MIT isn't at the top of any list. And although the men outnumber the women, the ratio between eligible men and women tends to be fairly even. Why is this? Because a good percentage of MIT men are more interested in computers, *Star Wars*, and classes. Don't worry, though, there are definitely standouts in both genders. For the most part, many students opt to try to meet people from other schools. Lots of guys will date girls from Boston University or Wellesley College. In fact, a lot of MIT girls have a tendency to be bitter towards the Wellesley girls who always show up at parties.

There is a fairly even number of relationships and hookups at MIT. What's more common? Well, it really depends who you are. Relationships range from totally random hookups to engagements by senior year. One of the biggest barriers to having a relationship at MIT is finding the time to have one. Many students compare the time commitment of a relationship to taking a lab class. Because of this, some people opt for hookups. At the same time, because MIT can be such a difficult place, many people find the need for a strong support system. Some people find this support in serious relationships.

The College Prowler® Grade on
Guys: C

A high grade for Guys indicates that the male population on campus is attractive, smart, friendly, and engaging, and that the school has a decent ratio of guys to girls.

The College Prowler® Grade on
Girls: C-

A high grade for Girls not only implies that the women on campus are attractive, smart, friendly, and engaging, but also that there is a fair ratio of girls to guys.

Athletics

The Lowdown On...
Athletics

Athletic Division:
Division III

Conference:
NEWMAC (New England
Men's and Women's
Athletic Conference)

School Mascot:
Beaver

**Males Playing
Varsity Sports:**
610 (25%)

**Females Playing
Varsity Sports:**
434 (24%)

→

Men's Varsity Sports:
Baseball
Basketball
Crew (Heavyweight)
Crew (Lightweight)
Cross-Country
Fencing
Football
Golf
Gymnastics
Ice Hockey
Lacrosse
Riffle
Sailing
Skiing
Soccer
Squash
Swimming
Tennis
Track & Field
Volleyball
Water Polo
Wrestling

Women's Varsity Sports:
Basketball
Crew (Lightweight)
Crew (On-Water Training)
Cross-Country
Field
Hockey
Lacrosse
Soccer
Softball
Swimming
Tennis
Track & Field
Volleyball

Club Sports:
Aikido
Archery
Badminton
Ballroom Dancing
Boxing
Cheerleading Club
Crew
Cricket
Cycling
Dance Troupe
Equestrian
Fencing
Field Hockey (Coed)
Figure Skating
Ice Hockey (Women)
Judo
Rifle/Pistol
Rugby (Men)
Rugby (Women)
Sailing
Scuba Club
Shotokan Karate
Snowboarding
Table Tennis
Tae Kwon Do Club
Ultimate Frisbee (Men)
Ultimate Frisbee (Women)
Volleyball (Men)
Volleyball (Women)
Volleyball (Intercollegiate)
Water Polo (Men)
Water Polo (Women)
Windsurfing
Volleyball

Athletic Fields

There is one astroturf field, outdoor track, and football field.

Getting Tickets

All games at MIT are free.

Most Popular Sports

Ultimate Frisbee

Best Place to Take a Walk

Esplanade Park

Gyms/Facilities

DuPont Gymnasium

The DuPont Gymnasium has a wooden floor that is both
basketball and volleyball compatible. Gymnastics equipment
is also set up at the far end of the gym.

Zesiger Center

The fitness center portion of Zesiger covers over 12,000
square feet. In the gym area, students can take advantage
of 65 pieces of cardiovascular equipment, an enhanced free
weight area, and a sports medicine center. There's also a
50-meter pool with 20 lanes, and one instructional pool with
six 25-yard lanes. Zesiger also has six international-sized,
glass-backed, state-of-the-art squash courts, as well as a
multi-purpose court that can be used for aerobics, basketball,
indoor soccer, volleyball, floor hockey, and more. Much of the
equipment at Zesiger is available for checkout.

Johnson Athletics Center

Located on the first floor of Johnson is an ice rink—as if Boston didn't have enough ice to go around—that is available for student use throughout the year. The ice rink has a concrete floor underneath, and it has permanent seating available for 1,200.

Located on the second floor, the facility has a rubberized track surface that is also lined for basketball and tennis courts. More courts are available in the Rockwell Cage section of Johnson. Here, there's a wooden floor which is marked for basketball, volleyball, and badminton.

Students Speak Out On...
Athletics

{ **"Varsity sports don't draw large crowds. On the whole, MIT sports rarely excel. Intramural (IM) sports are more popular because they are dorm or club organized, and there is no demand for practice time."**

Q "Given that we're all nerds, sports suck. I'm just kidding. **Most people on campus either participate in a varsity sport or intramural sports.**"

Q "**Athletics at MIT are up-and-coming.** MIT is starting to get better at providing athletes with the proper facilities, resources, and so on. However, the athletics department still has a long way to go."

Q "IM sports definitely dominate over varsity sports here at MIT. **There are so many sports available,** from the popular ones like football and soccer, to the smaller but still competitive, like table tennis and bowling. You can join teams by dorms, by Greek affiliation, or even by major. Everyone gets together and plays on different levels, but it's all for a good time. Varsity sports draw a decent crowd, but the MIT students are definitely no Big 10 fans. Still, we all go and cheer on our friends."

Q "**Sports are here, but they're not very important to most people's lives.** You can play if you like, but don't expect to be a super star for it. IM sports are a much bigger deal."

Q "People who play varsity think it's a big deal, but it tends to be overlooked by the general population. **Many people do IMs though, because you don't have to be good, and they're fun**."

Q "Varsity sports are big here in the sense that lots of people play, and it doesn't take over your life. **But in terms of spectators, almost no one watches games here**. MIT offers over 40 sports, so there's a pretty big variety. It can be as competitive as you want it to be. You can try something totally new and be successful at it. Some of our sports teams aren't so great since we're pretty big nerds."

Q "Sports exist. I don't participate, but **we have a bunch**."

Q "There are lots of sports teams that people play on. IM sports are pretty big. **Most people who play do it because they to do want something** that's not academic and they're not hardcore athletes."

Q "IM sports are really big. **We have a fairly content athletic community**, but MIT is just not that big on sports. We're Division III. I think we're good at crew, or rifle, or something. I've never been to a football game, in fact, I wasn't even aware we had a football team."

The College Prowler Take On...
Athletics

Although MIT is obviously not one of the most athletically competitive schools in the nation—or the Boston area for the matter—many students here are, in fact, very interested in sports. In fact, according to the NCAA, MIT offers one of the broadest intercollegiate athletic programs in the country. Even if MIT isn't necessarily winning championships, there are definitely more than enough sports for people to get involved in. Some varsity sports will take you even if you have never played before. Just be prepared to put in the work. Joining a varsity team means that you have to practice at least two hours a day. That's two hours less study time. As a result of the time they put into practices, though, athletes tend to be fairly good with their time management skills.

MIT also offers a wide variety of club and IM sports. IM sports are actually one of the favorite pastimes of MIT students. There are over 1000 IM teams with a 75 percent undergraduate participation rate. Most teams are organized through living groups, and IMs exist for everything from football to foosball. Again, if you're good, you can join one of the better leagues, but if you've never played before, there's usually a league for people like you, too. The great thing about IMs is that games are fairly infrequent, and they're a lot of fun.

The College Prowler® Grade on
Athletics: C+

A high grade in Athletics indicates that students have school spirit, that sports programs are respected, that games are well-attended, and that intramurals are a prominent part of student life.

Nightlife

The Lowdown On...
Nightlife

Club and Bar Prowler: Popular Nightlife Spots!

Avalon

15 Lansdowne Street

(617) 262-2424

www.avalonboston.com

Avalon was voted America's Most Popular Club at the 2005 Las Vegas Club Show Awards. This festive environment hosts a wide variety of DJs from all over the world. Sunday nights are 21-and-over, but on Thursday, Friday, and Saturday you only need to be over 19!

Axis

15 Lansdowne Street

(617) 262-2437

Axis is a techno club with a funky style. Partiers are encouraged to dress as crazily as they can; the more unusual the better. Sunday nights are gay nights, Monday nights, drag, and Saturday nights are X nights. With all of these fun themes, you'll find a wide variety of people at Axis.

Note: Avalon and Axis have recently merged into one giant nightclub, but still offer their own individual styles, drink prices, and music selection.

➜

Crossroads

495 Beacon Street

(617) 262-7371

www.crossroadsirishpub.com

Crossroads is an Irish Pub that offers food, drinks, entertainment, and games. While munching on some good food deals, such as "Pizza and a Pitcher," you can watch sporting events on TV or play darts at the bar upstairs. Crossroads offers a nice laid-back atmosphere on nights when the rest of the city is too crowded.

Embassy

41 Lansdowne Street

(617) 536-2100

The Embassy is a European-type club that offers both 19-and-over and 21-and-over nights. Drink prices are rather high, so bring your wallet.

Jake Ivory's

9 Lansdowne Street

(617) 247-1222

www.jakeivorys.com

Jake Ivory's is a dueling piano show, open Thursday, Friday, and Saturday. Two fantastic pianists sit opposite each other and play their hearts out on rock-n-roll songs from the '50s to the present.

Jillian's

145 Ipswich Street

(617) 437-0300

jilliansboston.com

Jillian's offers a great atmosphere for eating American food like burgers, sandwiches, and pizza, while hob-knobbing with celebrities such as Derek Jeter, Mark Walhberg, Clint Eastwood, or Sean Penn. They have 55 pool tables, virtual games, and six full bars.

Mama Kin

36 Lansdowne St

(617) 351-2525

This Boston club is located across from Fenway Park, and it is partially owned by Aerosmith. The club's mission is to promote local music, and the building is divided into two rooms which host two separate musical acts—local bands in the front room and big-name bands in the Lansdowne Street Music Hall. All shows are free, casual dress, and 21-and-over.

The Matrix

275 Tremont Street

(617) 542-4077

www.roxyboston.com

The Matrix is one of the many clubs in the Roxy complex. It has two rooms that offer different types of music. The Matrix also has underage nights, but the cover charge is higher for the youth.

Roxy

279 Tremont Street

(617) 338-ROXY, Ext. 7699

www.roxyboston.com

The Roxy is a nightclub complex with several different places to check out. They host concerts with guests that range from Peter Frampton to George Clinton, and they also have 18-and-over nights.

Bars Close At:

2 a.m.

Primary Areas with Nightlife:

Landsdowne Street (near Fenway Park)

The Theater District

Student Favorites:

Avalon/Axis

Crossroads

Other Places to Check Out:

An Tua Nua

Aria

Club Europa

Gypsy

Karma

Landsdowne Playhouse

Tequila Rain

Useful Resources for Nightlife:

www.stuffatnight.com

www.wickedparty.com

What to Do if You're Not 21:

A lot of Boston's nightclubs have under-21 nights. Unfortunately, they usually charge a higher cover for people under 21 because they can't buy drinks.

Favorite Drinking Games:

Beirut (Beer Pong)

Boat Races

Century Club

Quarters

Students Speak Out On...
Nightlife

"The parties rock, and they're open to everyone. Most weekends have three or more a night. There are also a lot of closed-party nights during the week at frats; you can go if you know the people there."

Q "I like Avalon a lot; we go to RiRa's (An Tua Nua) because it's cheap. I've been to Embassy, Lansdowne Playhouse, Club Europa, and Axis—they're all decent. **As far as bars are concerned, I am not really a big fan of them because they're expensive,** but I do have one particular favorite called Jake Ivory's Dueling Piano Bar."

Q "I have **no clue what the bars or the clubs are like,** sorry. I just don't get out much."

Q "**There are good clubs, but they're not as hot as New York City**. The clubbing scene here just does not compare. However, it is still pretty decent."

Q "Most of the parties are at the fraternities, and the dorms occasionally throw parties. The clubs are mostly located in Boston on Lansdowne. There are many bars located in both Boston and Cambridge. **The bar that most people go to is Crossroads,** which is on the corner of Beacon Street and Massachusetts Avenue."

Q **"There are tons of bars further into Cambridge—**
Central Square used to have the highest concentration of
nightspots in the Boston area. Avalon is good for the club
scene, though the frat parties are free."

Q "Frat parties are usually okay, although the scene does
get old after a while. If you're a freshman, you'll probably
think it's totally cool and fun. **Going frat hopping with
a bunch of friends never gets old though; crazy
adventures are yours for the making**. Clubs in Boston
are alright, though small and close early. Big name DJs
come to Boston to spin, so once in a while a club will
get packed, and it's fun. The clubs on Lansdowne Street
Avalon/Axis, Jillian's, and Karma reign the nightlife scene.
Roxy and the Matrix on Tremont Street are two good
places, also. For the older crowd, Aria and Gypsies are
more posh and exude a different vibe. Lots of bars are
scattered around; it's a good crowd usually."

Q "Clubs are 19-and-over, but they do have some 18-and-
over nights. **Parties on campus occur pretty frequently**,
especially at the beginning of the year."

Q "**Frat parties are fun for freshmen** to meet people en
masse. Clubs are good, but definitely borrow an ID
(a decent one) or get a fake because they're strict."

The College Prowler Take On...
Nightlife

You might think that because of the work, no one at MIT ever finds the time to party. And during the week, this is fairly common. In fact, some people even choose to work on weekends. But there is actually a large number of students who live by the motto "work hard, play hard." One of the main attractions on weekends for underclassmen is fraternity parties. They're free, and most are open to everyone. This includes people from all the surrounding schools. Parties can range from 500+ wall-to-wall people, to smaller, closed parties. Occasionally, certain dorms will also throw parties. This is usually where freshmen will go.

Unfortunately, most students tend to tire of fraternity parties after a couple of years. Luckily, there are many other options in Boston. For example, some people choose to go clubbing. Thursday night is actually one of the biggest nights to go out in Boston, and it is by far one of the best club nights. There are many clubs on Landsdowne. Some of the most popular include Avalon and Embassy. Most clubs are 19-and-over to keep out high school students. For the 21-and-over crowd, there are plenty of bars around Boston. One of the most popular with MIT students is Crossroads, located on Beacon Street.

The College Prowler® Grade on
Nightlife: A-

A high grade in Nightlife indicates that there are many bars and clubs in the area that are easily accessible and affordable. Other determining factors include the number of options for the under-21 crowd and the prevalence of house parties.

Greek Life

The Lowdown On...
Greek Life

**Number of
Fraternities:**
27

**Undergrad Men
in Fraternities:**
55%

**Number of
Sororities:**
5

**Undergrad Women
in Sororities:**
26%

➜

Fraternities on Campus:

Alpha Delta Phi
Alpha Epsilon Pi
Alpha Phi Alpha
Alpha Tau Omega
Beta Theta Pi
Chi Phi
Delta Kappa Epsilon
Delta Tau Delta
Delta Upsilon
Iota Upsilon Chapter
Kappa Alpha Psi
Kappa Sigma
Lambda Chi Alpha
Lambda Phi Epsilon
Nu Delta
Phi Beta Epsilon
Phi Delta Theta
Phi Kappa Sigma
Phi Kappa Theta
Phi Sigma Kappa
Pi Lambda Phi
Sigma Chi
Sigma Nu
Sigma Phi Epsilon
Tau Epsilon Phi
Theta Chi
Theta Delta Chi
Theta Xi
Zeta Beta Tau
Zeta Psi

Sororities on Campus:

Alpha Chi Omega
Alpha Epsilon Phi
Alpha Kappa Alpha
Alpha Phi Sorority
Kappa Alpha Theta
Sigma Kappa

Other Greek Organizations:

Interfraternity Council
Order of Omega
Panhellenic Council

Living Group Organizations:

Dormitory Council
Interfraternity Council
MIT Living Group Council

Independent Living Groups:

Epsilon Theta
Fenway House
Group (WILG)
No. 6 Club
Pika
Student House
Women's Independent Living

Students Speak Out On...
Greek Life

"Greek life is pretty cool here. There's a lot going on if you want to be involved in it, and plenty of other things to do if you don't. They certainly know how to throw really good parties."

Q "It doesn't dominate the social scene because there isn't just one social scene, there are several. How much you get involved in them **depends entirely on your preferences and desires**. MIT Greeks are non-standard, by the way. Some are stereotypical frats and sororities, but we also have an assortment of atypical fraternities and independent living groups. Many of those are dry (no alcohol), and they frequently have their own style. Check out Epsilon Theta, Pika, Fenway House, and WILG for an idea."

Q "Greek life is awesome! **I think most of the social scene is provided by Greek life**."

Q "Greek life is prevalent, but it doesn't dominate the social scene. If you decide to participate, then it can become your only scene, **but having a social life is not dependent on fraternities or sororities**."

Q **"Greek life here is not the Greek life you see on TV**! You don't have to pay to get into parties. Frats have lots of parties with DJs and stuff, so it's fun."

Q "Everyone who comes to MIT is a nerd, and that's the bottom line. Frat guys can act like they're all hardcore, but they're really not. **There's no way to describe MIT Greek life—it just isn't like it is at big state universities**. It's more like another option for living rather than a system that takes over the social scene."

Q "Greek life is pretty big at MIT. The frats and sororities don't follow the typical stereotypes at other schools. For the most part, they have a very positive impact on campus. **Sometimes it feels like it controls the social scene**, but there is still a lot to do without getting involved in Greek life. MIT is basically in Boston, so everybody can find something they like to do."

Q "It's very popular. **The frats here are different than other places, though they still like to party**. They mostly live off campus in gorgeous brownstones. The sororities are huge—like 100 people—and most have housing. They're a lot of fun and not catty like that MTV show."

The College Prowler Take On...
Greek Life

As with everything else at MIT, the personalities of the fraternities and sororities vary. Everyone who wants to join can usually find some place where they feel comfortable. Many of the fraternities and sororities have gorgeous houses for great prices in the heart of Boston. If you're concerned about the distance, some even have houses on dorm row. One unique thing about MIT's Greek life is the existence of another set of houses called the Independent Living Groups. Although they're not Greek, they still provide places to live, and they have historically been grouped with the fraternities and sororities. However, the ILGs are actually very distinct entities, and they are very vehement about being different from the Greeks.

With 27 fraternities and 5 sororities, MIT has an incredibly vibrant Greek system. Fraternities usually have between 25-50 brothers, and most sororities have about 100 sisters. The percentage of men who join fraternities is higher than the percentage of women who join sororities. But this isn't Greek life like you see on TV. Greek life at MIT revolves more around academics and building friendships than pure social activities. Many community service events are sponsored or attended by Greek houses, and Greeks also hold many leadership positions. The Greek system at MIT is unlike what most people would expect at other schools. That is why many of the people who go Greek at MIT are people who never would have considered it at any other school.

The College Prowler® Grade on
Greek Life: A

A high grade in Greek Life indicates that sororities and fraternities are not only present, but also active on campus. Other determining factors include the variety of houses available and the respect the Greek community receives from the rest of the campus.

Drug Scene

The Lowdown On...
Drug Scene

Most Prevalent Drugs on Campus:
Alcohol

Marijuana

Drug Counseling Programs:
AA – Alcoholics Anonymous
Open to the public
Room E23-364
Monday 5:30 p.m.–6:30 p.m.
Tuesday 12 p.m.–1 p.m.
Thursday 12 p.m.–1 p.m.
Call (617) 253-4911 for more information.

Alcohol Support Group
MIT students only
Wednesday 7:30 a.m.– 9:00 a.m.
Room E23-364

Call (617) 253-4911 to make an appointment before attending this group.

Counseling and Support Services
(617) 253-4861

Narcotics Anonymous Helpline
(617) 884-7709

Students Speak Out On...
Drug Scene

{ **"It's as big as you want it to be—if you want to get drugs, you can, but if you want to avoid them, it's just as easy."**

Q "I cannot comment on the drug scene because I am not a part of it. I do have friends that are, but not heavily. There are drugs here at MIT, but they don't rule everyone's life. **As far as I know, MIT has never really had much of a problem with drug abuse**."

Q "The drug scene **depends entirely on where you live**."

Q "Alcohol is definitely the most prevalent drug on campus, if you choose to classify it as one. Aside from that, pot would come in second. I know people who are involved in that and some other people who deal with heavier drugs, but most do not let their habits affect their schoolwork. **For a lot of the people who choose to do drugs, it's merely a social routine**."

Q "**No, there's not really a drug scene**."

Q "As far as drugs, alcohol, or anything else goes, it's all there. **Sure, it's college, but it's not in your face**. If you like it, you can find it; if you don't, you don't ever have to deal with it."

Q "**There are actually several users scattered through a couple of dorms**. Just ask when you get here; it's one of those open secrets. There are people who will strongly discourage the harder drugs, but the soft ones are quite common."

The College Prowler Take On...
Drug Scene

Some people do use drugs at MIT. A surprising number of students use marijuana occasionally or have at least tried it. It is the most widely used drug, and users have an easy enough time getting their hands on it. After all, MIT is right in Boston, and as with any other urban area, drugs are there for those who want them. But one of the unique aspects of the drug scene at MIT is that even those people who use drugs tend to know when they need to do work. Stories of students becoming so addicted to drugs that they fail out of school are rare. After all, students aren't paying all that money on tuition for nothing. Most people know that, in the end, they are at MIT to get one of the best educations in the world.

For those who have no desire to do drugs, you will never be forced to. And avoiding the drug scene is not hard. Even under peer pressure, you should not feel uncomfortable simply saying "no." People respect each other's choices here. The bottom line at MIT is that students are given a large amount of freedom to make their own decisions, and they take responsibility for them.

The College Prowler® Grade on
Drug Scene: B+

A high grade in the Drug Scene indicates that drugs are not a noticeable part of campus life; drug use is not visible, and no pressure to use them seems to exist.

Campus Strictness

The Lowdown On...
Campus Strictness

What Are You Most Likely to Get Caught Doing on Campus?

- Being too loud (noise violations)
- Various alcohol-related offenses

Students Speak Out On...
Campus Strictness

{
"Campus police don't do anything other than shut down parties due to noise complaints. Unless something happens due to drugs or drinking—someone getting hurt—then they'll definitely do something."

Q "Campus police [CPs] crash parties frequently to ensure that facilities are not overcrowded and that minors are not consuming alcohol. Although in my experience, CPs have never arrested anyone or gotten anyone in serious trouble with drugs or drinking. I have seen people get taken away in ambulances for their own safety. Most of the time, the **CPs are just there for the benefit of the students**, to keep people in line, and to make sure it's safe."

Q "**It's not very strict**. It depends where you live and what kind of an environment you're looking for. Some dorms are very free, others are strict."

Q "I don't know about their view on drugs, but the CPs are **relatively lax about drinking**. Fraternities only need to register their parties and they are the ones responsible for the amount of alcohol the partygoers consume. The CPs generally do not intervene with parties unless there is a major incident."

Q "In light of the death of a student in 1995 due to drinking, Administrators are strict on alcohol. But **if you want to get wasted, it's really still very easy**."

Q "The campus police are **very strict when it comes to drugs and drinking**. If you are found using drugs, or if you are underage and drunk or found consuming alcohol, you will face disciplinary action. I don't know how far they would go with the punishments; I have never seen it happen in my years here. I do know that they state the policy and print it in the school material if you do decide to come here. There is also a CD sent to you that deals with alcohol, although it's mainly for your parents' viewing."

Q "I've never quite found out how strict campus police are about drinking. **Most resident assistants (RAs) don't really mind**, as long as it is not out of control."

Q "Are they strict? **Only if you get caught doing something stupid**. The rest of the time, the school doesn't seem to care."

Q "Campus police are **generally more strict on fraternities than the dorms** in terms of drinking. I have never heard of any students getting busted for drugs. Don't expect to be able to bring a handle to class, but it's definitely within easy access if you want to get trashed."

The College Prowler Take On...
Campus Strictness

Any discussion of campus strictness at MIT has to include the fact that a freshman died in an alcohol-related incident several years ago. In the wake of this event, the MIT administration has made many changes in policies regarding freshmen, housing, and alcohol in the past few years. As a result, penalties and punishments for alcohol- and drug-related infractions can be harsh. But the MIT administration generally doesn't punish individuals. In general, MIT will try to punish the living group where the student was drinking or taking the drugs. The punishments can be anything from prohibiting alcohol at the house, to losing the actual housing license. Therefore, living groups, especially fraternities, tend to be as careful as possible.

These punishments only apply if you get caught, and most individuals are not caught. As for parties, campus police are most likely to respond to complaints about noise. (Parties are required to end at 1 a.m. in Cambridge.) The campus police can be strict or not, depending on the living group. If you're an underage student consuming alcohol, just avoid the CPs, and you'll be left alone. Definitely be cautious at parties, though, and practice common sense at all times.

B-

The College Prowler® Grade on

Campus
Strictness: B-

A high Campus Strictness grade implies an overall lenient atmosphere; police and RAs are fairly tolerant, and the administration's rules are flexible.

Parking

The Lowdown On...
Parking

Approximate Parking Permit Cost:

Commuter Students
$410 per year

Resident Students
$592 per year

Student Carpool
$205 per year

Student Parking Lot?

Yes

MIT Parking and Transportation Office:

(617) 258-6510
mitparking@mit.edu

Common Parking Tickets:

Expired Meter: $20
No Parking Zone: $30
Fire Lane: $40
Handicapped Zone: $50

Freshmen Allowed to Park?

No

Students Speak Out On...
Parking

{ **"Parking is pretty difficult and expensive on campus. Most students try parking on the Memorial Drive next to campus, but it is sometimes hard to find parking. I don't recommend driving."**

Q "Student parking is available on campus, but I really wouldn't bring my car to Boston. **Public transportation is way more efficient**."

Q "Don't bother unless you're **very patient or insane**."

Q "**Having a car in Boston is not a good idea**. It's okay, but you don't really need it."

Q "**It is very easy to park**. I brought my car up here as a sophomore; freshmen aren't allowed to have cars on campus. You can pay to park in the MIT lots, which are very expensive, or you can park on the streets for free. I chose not to pay for parking, and I park my car right outside of my dorm, so it's not far away."

Q "**Parking around Boston is generally hectic**, but there are places. I always know where to direct people to park their cars, and it never costs money."

Q "Parking around campus is by permit only. Maybe you can get away with it once or twice, but you'll just end up getting towed if you do it too often. Like everywhere else around Cambridge and Boston, it's **probably easier to get a bike or just rely on public transportation**."

Q "You shouldn't bring a car. **Parking is a nightmare—it is the same with driving**."

Q "It's not great. You can get passes, but **you probably don't want a car** unless you're planning on driving back home a lot."

Q "I don't have a car, but **it seems painful** to have one."

The College Prowler Take On...
Parking

When you have to move a lot of heavy things, or when you have a craving for IHOP at 4 a.m., there's nothing better than having your own car. In general, having a car can be a great convenience so that you don't have to take public transportation. Technically, if you want to get a parking sticker, you have to be an upperclassman. But getting a parking sticker can be expensive, and even then, finding an open spot in the lot is difficult. If you don't have a sticker, parking your car on campus can be a nightmare. There are several lots on campus, but many require permits at certain times of day. Some students opt to not get permits, but they end up paying that amount back in parking tickets. Beware: you will get towed if you are parked anywhere near a no parking zone.

Your best bets for parking around campus are the Westgate lot by Next House, parking on Vassar Street near Simmons, or parking in the Kresge lot (only nights and weekends). Students also park on Memorial Drive. Off campus, parking in Boston is difficult, as well. Street parking is metered, and garage parking is expensive. Moreover, sometimes parking is so crowded that you have to park far, far away from your destination. However, many of the FSILGs do have their own parking lots.

The College Prowler® Grade on

Parking: C-

A high grade in this section indicates that parking is both available and affordable, and that parking enforcement isn't overly severe.

Transportation

The Lowdown On...
Transportation

Ways to Get Around Town:

On Campus
EZ Ride
SafeRide
Tech Shuttle

Public Transportation
Subway - $22 per month
Bus - $12 per month

Taxi Cabs
Cambridge:
Ambassador Brattle Cab
(617) 492-1100
Cambridge Cab Company
(617) 498-0006
Cambridge Taxi
(617) 492-7900
Checker Cab Company
(617) 497-1500
Yellow Cab
(617) 876-5000

→

(Taxi Cabs, continued)

Boston:

Boston Cab
(617) 536-5010

Checker Cab
(617) 536-7000

City Cab
(617) 536-5100

Metro Cab
(617) 782-5500

Car Rentals

Alamo
local (617) 561-4100
national (800) 327-9633
www.alamo.com

Avis
local (617) 569-8890
national (800) 831-2847
www.avis.com

Budget
local (617) 497-1801
national (800) 527-0700
www.budget.com

Dollar
local (617) 723-2065
national (800) 800-4000
www.dollar.com

Enterprise
local (617) 262-8222
national (800) 736-8222
www.enterprise.com

Hertz
local (617) 569-7272
national (800) 654-3131
www.hertz.com

National
local (617) 569-6700
national (800) 227-7368
www.nationalcar.com

Best Ways to Get Around Town

MBTA service: T (operates both above and underground), bus lines (follows T lines around the city), MBTA rails (runs between cities around Massachusetts), biking/blading along the river, taxi service.

Ways to Get

Out of Town:

Airport

Logan International Airport, (617) 567-7844. The airport is approximately 20 minutes driving time from MIT.

Airlines Serving Boston (Logan Airport)

Aer Lingus 1-800-IRISH AIR
www.aerlingus.com

Air Canada 1-888-247-2262
www.aircanada.com

Air France 1-800-237-2747
www.airfrance.com

Air Tran 1-800-AIRTRAN
www.airtran.com

Alaska Airlines 1-800-252-5522
www.alaskaair.com

Alitalia 1-800-223-5730
www.alitaliausa.com

America West 1-800-235-9292
www.americawest.com

American Airlines
1-800-433-7300
www.aa.com

British Airways 1-800-AIRWAYS
www.britishairways.com

Cape Air 1-800-352-0714
www.flycapeair.com

(Airlines, continued)

Continental 1-800-523-3273
www.continental.com

Delta Airlines 1-800-221-1212
www.delta-air.com

Icelandair 1-800-223-5500
www.icelandair.com

KLM 1-800-374-7747
www.klm.com

Lufthansa 1-800-645-3880
www.lufthansa.com

Midwest 1-800-452-2022
www.midwestexpress.com

Northwest 1-800-225-2525
www.nwa.com

Qantas 1-800-227-4500
www.qantas.com.au

SATA 1-800-762-9995
www.sata.pt

Song 1-800-221-1212
www.flysong.com

Swiss 1-877-359-7947
www.swiss.com

TACA 1-800-535-8780
www.taca.com

United 1-800-241-6522
www.united.com

US Airways 1-800-428-4322
www.usairways.com

Virgin Atlantic 1-800-862-8621
www.fly.virgin.com

How to Get to the Airport

Take the subway or a cab.
A cab ride to the airport
costs about $20-$30,
depending on traffic.

Buslines

Bonanza Bus Lines
1-888-751-8800
www.bonanzabus.com
Bonanza Buslines–South
Station Bus Terminal
700 Atlantic Avenue
Boston, MA 02110
(617) 720-4110

Greyhound
1-800-229-9424
www.greyhound.com
South Station Bus Terminal
700 Atlantic Avenue
Boston, MA 02110
(617) 526-1801

Peter Pan Bus Lines
1-800-343-9999
www.peterpanbus.com
South Station Bus Terminal
700 Atlantic Avenue
Boston, MA 02110

Amtrak

Amtrak
1-800-USA-RAIL
www.amtrak.com
Back Bay Station
145 Dartmouth Street
Boston, MA 02116

Travel Agents

STA Travel
Student Center
(617) 225-2555

Getting Around Campus

There are a couple things you should know about getting around MIT's campus. First, most of the classrooms are connected to one primary building. This may not make sense to you, but think of it as a typical high school building, except much bigger, and everything was built in different eras, in completely different styles. This means that on any given day, you can go to all of your classes without ever going outside. Another particularly eccentric thing about MIT's class buildings is that, although some buildings are named after people, they are rarely called by their given names. Like so many other things at MIT, the buildings have a representative number system. The individual buildings are referred to by their assigned number, though they *are not* in chronological order. So, don't expect Building 3 to be next to Building 2 because it's not. This number system is not something that can easily be explained, so just make sure to have a map on you at all times when you first get to campus. There's no shame in having to consult a map—few newcomers *ever* know where they are.

MIT does provide a decent number of transportation services on campus. These include the Tech Shuttle and the SafeRide. The Tech Shuttle runs during the daytime hours on a route as far east as Kendall Square, and as far west as Tang Hall (right next to Next House). SafeRide runs after 6 p.m. and goes to the various dorms and living groups around Cambridge and Boston. Both services run frequently, and MIT now runs a GPS system called ShuttleTrack, so you can see where each one is at any given time. Check out *http://shuttletrack.mit.edu.*

Students Speak Out On...
Transportation

{ **"Boston's public transportation system is wonderful. Buses, subways, and trains connect you with almost every corner of Boston and its surrounding suburbs."**

Q "The transportation is very good, but it's not as good as New York City or DC. **The T is kind of ghetto—not dangerous-ghetto, but dirty-ghetto**."

Q "**Public transportation is great**. There is a bus stop right in front of the school, a subway stop on one end of campus, and free shuttles to the mall and to the frats located throughout Boston."

Q "Public transportation mainly consists of the T. MIT has its own T stop. **It's very useful, and it's the best way to get around Boston**."

Q "There is bus and subway transportation that's **adequate for getting to most places around Boston**."

Q "**One thing I love about Boston is the ease of its public transportation system**. MIT is located five minutes from a subway station, and there are bus stops right next to the student center. The buses, subway, and commuter rail are all connected. You can go anywhere on them."

Q "**It's wonderful—always use public transportation**. There isn't parking for cars, and there is always traffic."

Q "Public transportation is very convenient. **The main bus has a stop at MIT, and it can take you further into Cambridge or into Boston**. It connects to many of the T stops. The T is the train service here. There is also a T stop on campus, although it is in East Campus."

Q "I think public transportation is great. **You don't need a car to go anywhere**."

The College Prowler Take On...
Transportation

Learning the public transportation system is one of the keys to fully enjoying Boston. There are two main options: the subway (called the T) and buses. There are two T stops in and around campus. One is in Kendall Square, and the other is up Massachusetts Avenue in Central Square. Although there are various bus stops around campus, the main ones are at 77 and 84 Mass. Avenue.

Buses tend to run more frequently, but learning which bus goes where can be a pain. Many students will never ride anything other than the 1 and the CT1 buses that go up and down Mass. Avenue. Moreover, buses can often be delayed by traffic at certain times of day. On the other hand, the T is never delayed by traffic. However, there are fewer routes, but the buses tend to be cleaner. If you use public transportation frequently, you should consider buying a bus and/or T pass through MIT. The discount for students is 50 percent. In any case, public transportation will take you anywhere you want to go around Boston, and it's cheap. Although some of the facilities could be nicer, few are disappointed with the system.

The College Prowler® Grade on

Transportation: A

A high grade for Transportation indicates that campus buses, public buses, cabs, and rental cars are readily-available and affordable. Other determining factors include proximity to an airport and the necessity of transportation.

Weather

The Lowdown On...
Weather

Average Temperature:
Fall: 54 °F
Winter: 29 °F
Spring: 48 °F
Summer: 74 °F

Average Precipitation:
Fall: 3.37 in.
Winter: 3.63 in.
Spring: 3.70 in.
Summer: 3.23 in.

Students Speak Out On...
Weather

{ **"Bring clothes for all weather types. Students must learn to check *weather.com* every morning, because the weather can, and will, change within hours."**

Q "So far, it's been erratic. The winter has been pretty brutal this year, while the year before it was quite mild. Bring everything from shorts and tank tops, to ski jackets and hats because **you might need it all**—maybe even within the same month."

Q "**Best thing to do is layer**. If you are from the West Coast, buy your jacket, sweaters, and boots here."

Q "**Today it's sunny, tomorrow it will snow**, and next week we'll have 90-degree-in-the-shade weather."

Q "**New England weather is crazy**. One day, it's 90 degrees out; the next day, there's snow on the ground."

Q "New England weather is unpredictable, so **pack for all four seasons**. In the fall, long pants and a shirt with a jacket will keep you toasty. In the winter, wrap on a thick down jacket and slap on some ear muffs. The cutting wind, snow, and sleet, and the occasional blizzards will also require you to wear some tough boots. In the spring, do not forget to bring your umbrella. And if you stay for the summer, equip yourself with minimal attire: shorts, tank tops, flip flops, and an air conditioner."

Q "New England weather is very different. Going into fall, it gets colder and colder, but once we get through winter and spring comes, it is very nice. Because we are right next to the Charles River, our weather varies throughout the day. **It can be cold in the morning, get warmer by mid-day, and get cold again in a few hours**. Then it will get warmer again by nightfall. It gets hard when it comes to dressing appropriately for the weather, but we never get anything too extreme. Since I'm from New York, I kind of knew what to expect."

Q "**The heat, haze, and humidity will probably make you want to crawl inside a freezer**. Looking at the bigger picture, Boston's fall foliage, wintery snowfall, spring flowers, and summer sunshine are all actually quite nice."

The College Prowler Take On...
Weather

Weather is one of the MIT students' greatest gripes (next to work). The reason is that you simply never know what it's going to be like on any given day. Temperatures can range from below zero freezing in the winter, to high 80s and humid in the summer. During the school year, the weather is usually fairly cold. If you've never lived through cold weather before, be prepared for a shock. Basically, be sure to bring a wide variety of clothes. But the things that you absolutely need are a thick winter coat, waterproof shoes, and a hat. There is nothing worse then watching Californians trying to struggle through that first cold week without enough winter clothing. Fortunately, most of the MIT class buildings are all connected. So depending on where you live, you may not have to be in the cold for very long. And even if it was freezing rain when you walked to class in the morning, it could be sunny and clear by the time you leave to go home in the afternoon.

Despite the temperatures, try to get out and play at least once in a while. Usually on the night of the first snowfall, students abandon their studies to play snow football or have snowball fights. One recent winter, MIT even had a snow day! Don't count on that happening too often, but it's at least something to hope for.

The College Prowler® Grade on
Weather: C-

A high Weather grade designates that temperatures are mild and rarely reach extremes, that the campus tends to be sunny rather than rainy, and that weather is fairly consistent rather than unpredictable.

Report Card Summary

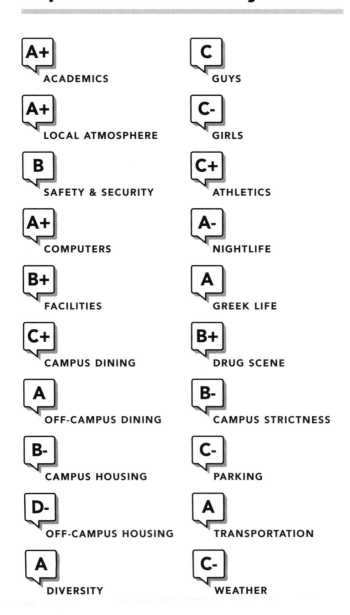

A+
ACADEMICS

C
GUYS

A+
LOCAL ATMOSPHERE

C-
GIRLS

B
SAFETY & SECURITY

C+
ATHLETICS

A+
COMPUTERS

A-
NIGHTLIFE

B+
FACILITIES

A
GREEK LIFE

C+
CAMPUS DINING

B+
DRUG SCENE

A
OFF-CAMPUS DINING

B-
CAMPUS STRICTNESS

B-
CAMPUS HOUSING

C-
PARKING

D-
OFF-CAMPUS HOUSING

A
TRANSPORTATION

A
DIVERSITY

C-
WEATHER

Overall Experience

Students Speak Out On...
Overall Experience

{ **"We get our hands dirty, we work together, and sometimes we fail together. Personally, I think you'll have a much greater chance of figuring out who you really are and what you really want to do with yourself if you come to MIT."**

Q "It's been an incredible experience: challenging academics, wonderful people, and actually some fun occasionally. There are a few days each term where you say to yourself, **'If I had gone to state school, I would be partying instead of studying right now.'** But despite the stress, I can't picture myself anywhere else. This is where I belong."

Q "I'm satisfied with my college experience. I'm not satisfied with my academic experience. I'm leaving here pretty burnt-out and somewhat unsure of my abilities in the real world. **MIT arms you with a lot of educational tools and the ability to learn**, but it takes about four years to regain your confidence and self-esteem."

Q "Only come to MIT if you know that's where you want to go. MIT prides itself on a rigorous curriculum. Know that when you come here, you'll be doing a lot more studying than you did in high school. Know that there may not always be time to go to a party because you have a problem set due soon, and you need to spend a lot of time working on it. Just know that by coming to MIT, you are **sacrificing some of your social life to put in a hard four years of work**. Then, when you graduate, you can look back and truly appreciate what MIT did for you."

Q "It rocks. It's really tough—you'll hate it, but you'll love it. **IHTFP is the local motto**—it has a double meaning of 'I have truly found paradise,' and 'I hate this #$%-ing place,' and we mean every word of it. The culture around here tends to subdivide; the vast majority of students are friendly, but the pressure creates smaller, close-knit groups. Some of them are centered on living groups, some are based on extracurricular activities, and others are just gangs of friends. But even the social life here tends to be more intense as a result of all of the academic stress."

Q "I love MIT, and I love Boston. **The only thing that would make this place better is better-looking women**."

Q "I have enjoyed almost every moment of my experience at MIT. Despite all the work and stress, **my two years at this crazy institute of learning have been tremendously rewarding and satisfying**. Living on my own and supporting myself through school has taught me a lot about life, as well. The people I have met at MIT have been amazing. I would not want to be anywhere else."

Q "Its hard, but worth it. **I sometimes wish it were easier, but then, it wouldn't be MIT**, would it?"

Q "I love MIT because of the people I've met, but I've struggled with my original decision to come here after spending four years studying something I don't like. I should've gone somewhere else, but I chose MIT because of the people and the environment. **I wanted to be all hardcore and stuff**. (Sigh) Silly me."

Q "It gets better as you go along. **The longer I'm here, the luckier I feel**."

The College Prowler Take On...
Overall Experience

MIT students have a love/hate relationship with their school. They love the people and the atmosphere, and hate the boatloads of work. Correction, some people like the work and learning things, but most people hate being ignored by certain "research-oriented" professors. Most of the students who attend MIT had some tough decisions to make about schools. For example, "Should I go to Harvard or MIT?" or, "Should I go to this in-state school with a full scholarship and a free computer, or go to MIT and pay for almost everything?" Overall, every student, at some point, will think that they made the wrong decision. But it's the fact that these people made the decision to attend MIT that sets them apart from the rest. Whether they knew what the school was like or not, students here were willing to take the chance. As a result, the people at MIT are the most creative, helpful, brilliant, and unique in the world. MIT admissions doesn't admit people accidentally (no matter how dumb you may feel when you fail your first exam). Everyone at MIT is incredibly down-to-earth, and everyone has the potential to do great things, even if we are all deprived of sleep. It's okay—you'll find that some of the best work happens between 3 a.m. and 5 a.m.

MIT will teach you how to survive on your own in the real world. It will teach you more about yourself, too. Don't expect to be babied. MIT is one of the most challenging schools in the country, but it is also one of the most rewarding. It is an opportunity that few are given, so don't waste your time. While you are here, you will grow up and become an adult. You will form some life-long relationships, and if you survive, you will thrive anywhere.

The Inside Scoop

The Lowdown On...
The Inside Scoop

MIT Slang

Know the slang, know the school! The following is a list of things you really need to know before coming to MIT. The more of these words you know, the better off you'll be.

MIT students don't refer to majors by their names (i.e. management or electrical engineering). Instead, the majors are referred to by the following "course numbers."

1 – Civil and Environmental Engineering

2 – Mechanical Engineering

3 – Materials Science and Engineering

4 – Architecture

5 – Chemistry

6 – Computer Science and Electrical Engineering

7 – Biology

8 – Physics

9 – Brain and Cognitive Sciences

10 – Chemical Engineering

11 – Urban Studies and Planning

12 – Earth, Atmospheric, and Planetary Sciences

13 – Ocean Engineering

14 – Economics

15 – Management

→

(MIT Slang, continued)

16 – Aeronautics and Astronautics

17 – Political Science

18 – Mathematics

21 – Humanities

22 – Nuclear Engineering

24 – Philosophy and Linguistics

6.001 – The introductory Computer Science/Electrical Engineering course known for its intensity.

Athena – The school computer system.

IFC – Interfraternity Council, the governing body for the fraternities.

FEE – Freshmen Essay Evaluation.

FPOP – Freshman Pre-Orientation Program.

FSILG – Fraternities Sororities and Independent Living Groups.

F*%# Truck – The bus that goes between MIT and Wellesley College.

Hack – Harmless but clever—often large-scale—practical jokes that MIT students pull.

IHTFP – I Hate This %&^@-ing Place, though there are many variations on this definition.

Lobby 10 – The lobby that opens out to Killian Court. Students do various advertising and fundraising activities here.

Mass. Ave – Massachusetts Avenue.

Punt – Not doing your work.

Rush – Period where FSILGs recruit new members.

SafeRide – The nighttime shuttle that goes to dorms and FSILGs in Boston and Cambridge.

SPAMIT – Stupid People At MIT.

Sloan – MIT's business school.

T – The subway system.

Tech Shuttle – A daytime shuttle that runs between Tang Hall and Kendall Square.

Tooling – Doing school work, (i.e. problem sets, papers, or studying for tests).

UROP – Undergraduate Research Opportunities Program. This tends to be one of the most common jobs on campus.

Z-Center – Zesiger Center, MIT's main athletic facility.

Zephyr – An Athena-based instant messaging program.

Things I Wish I Knew Before Coming to MIT

Consider learning the Greek alphabet. With so many fraternities and sororities, it's bound to come in handy at some point. If you ever see a random group of letters written on a desk, there's probably some member of a fraternity or living group responsible.

Tips to Succeed at MIT

- Do a Pre-Orientation Program. The people who do these always end up knowing the campus better, and having a built-in group of friends before orientation even starts. You're just a step ahead if you decide to do this. In fact, FLP (Freshman Leadership Program) is one of the largest, most popular programs at MIT.

- Realize that you might not be the best/smartest anymore. You're actually being compared to people who are just as smart—if not smarter—than you are. Don't be disappointed, be content that you are truly in a group of your peers.

- Start your work as early as possible. There's nothing worse than having to pull a last minute all-nighter before something is due. By doing your work in little increments, you'll actually end up with more free time. And studying for tests will be easier because you've been working at it frequently.

- Sometimes, you can't do all the work that you are assigned Learn to prioritize. Better yet, learn to deal.

- Work in groups. Sure, you'll get more glory if you do everything by yourself, but you also might end up in a padded room.

- Meet as many people as possible during orientation. The campus is really vibrant and friendly up until the first round of tests during the third and fourth weeks.

- Don't believe everything you hear. Sometimes a rumor about a class, professor, or friend is nothing more than that, a rumor.

School Spirit

When it comes to school spirit, most students have a love/hate relationship with MIT, and "spirit" is focused more within housing communities, than it is within the overall University structure. Students have a fierce pride in their living groups.

Traditions

Hacks

Look for them around campus. Some of the most famous include an MIT balloon inflating in the middle of the field during Harvard/ Yale football game, a cow on top of the dome, a house on top of the dome, and many others.

Killian Kickoff

This is the traditional kickoff party for FSILG rush period. It used to be held right at the end of orientation, but the date has varied throughout the past few years.

Steer Roast

This is a weekend-long event held at Senior House, including bands, mud wrestling, body painting and, of course, the roasting of a steer.

Spring Weekend

One of the last weekends in April featuring an international fair, a concert, and many other activities.

CPW (Campus Preview Weekend)

This is a weekend for prospective freshmen (prospies) to come visit MIT and see what they think.

IAP (Independent Activities Period)

This is the month between semesters where MIT students have the chance to do whatever they want!

Bad Taste

Bad taste is an annual concert held by the Chorallaries, an MIT singing group. The concert occurs late at night to accommodate its reputation for being "in bad taste."

Finding a Job or Internship

The Lowdown On...
Finding a Job or Internship

Advice

Start early, and don't get discouraged. Make your resume as soon as possible, and take it to the career services office. They offer free resume critiques. Post it on MonsterTRAK. Check MonsterTRAK often. Don't be afraid to pick up the phone and call certain companies. Even more than that, don't be afraid to contact alumni. MIT has a great alumni network that you should take advantage of. You may be worried that alumni will get annoyed with a lot of people calling and e-mailing them, but the truth is that few students actually do this. Therefore, if you do, you will be showing great initiative.

Career Center Resources & Services

Office of Career Services and Pre-Professional Advising

(617) 253 - 4733

http://web.mit.edu/career

Grads Who Enter the Job Market Within

6 months: 35%

1 Year: N/A

Firms That Most Frequently Hire Graduates

McKinsey, Microsoft, MIT, Oracle, Goldman Sachs,
IBM, Boston Consulting Group, Northrup Grumman,
Bain & Company

Alumni

The Lowdown On...
Alumni

Web Site:
http://alum.mit.edu

E-Mail:
aacomments@mit.edu

Office:
Association of Alumni and Alumnae of MIT

77 Massachusetts Ave., 10-110 Cambridge, MA 02139-4307

1-800-MIT-1865

Services Available:
Free subscription to *Technology Review*

Infinite Connection – Alumni network online

Library, sports, and athletics resources

MIT Alumni ID

→

Major Alumni Events

Alumni Travel Program

MIT Club meetings

Reunions

Alumni Publications

Technology Review

Did You Know?

Famous MIT Alums

George L. Eastman (Class of 1870) – Founder, Eastman Kodak

John T. Dorrance (Class of 1895) – Founder, Campbell Soup Company

Cecil H. Green (Class of '23) – Founder, Texas Instruments

William R. Hewlett SM (Class of '36) – Founder, Hewlett Packard Company

Amar G. Bose (Class of '51) – Founder, Bose Corporation

Edwin "Buzz" Aldrin (Class of '62) – Second man to walk on the moon

Robert Metcalfe (Class of '68) – Inventor of the Ethernet and founder of 3Com Corporation

Benjamin Netanyahu (Class of '75) – Youngest elected Prime Minister of Israel

There are **too many MIT alumni to list**. In addition, MIT alumni win a significant number of Nobel prizes. Just know that MIT alumni have been known to achieve incredible things.

In a study released by BankBoston and MIT entitled *MIT: The Impact of Innovation*, the effects of MIT alumni were calculated in terms of economic impact. The study reported that in the mid '90s, MIT graduates were responsible for creating firms that employed 1.1 million people and generated $232 billion in world sales.

Student Organizations

There are over 330 student grganizations at MIT. If you find a club you like, check out at the Web site listed or go to *http://web.mit.edu/life/index.html* for a complete listing of Web sites.

Comedy

Plush Daddy Fly: *http://web.mit.edu/plush/www*

Roadkill Buffet: *http://web.mit.edu/roadkill/www*

Russian Improv Comedy Team (KBH): *http://web.mit.edu/kbh*

Competition

Chess Club: *http://chess-club.mit.edu*

Debate Team: *http://web.mit.edu/debate/www*

Entrepreneurship Competition ($50K): *http://50k.mit.edu*

IAP Mystery Hunt: *http://web.mit.edu/puzzle/www*

MIT Go Club: *http://web.mit.edu/mitgoclub/www*

MIT Sloan eBusiness Awards: *http://www.mitawards.org*

MIT/Draper Labs Bridge Club: *http://web.mit.edu/mitdlbc/www/home.html*

Model United Nations Society: *http://web.mit.edu/mun*

Quiz Bowl Team: *http://web.mit.edu/collegebowl/www*

Dance

Argentine Tango Club: *http://web.mit.edu/tango/www*

Ballroom Dance Club: *http://web.mit.edu/bdclub*

Ballroom Dance Team: *http://mitbdt.mit.edu*

Casino Rueda Group: *http://web.mit.edu/rueda/www*

Dance Mix Coalition: *http://web.mit.edu/mitdmc/www*

Dance Troupe: *http://web.mit.edu/dancetroupe/www*

Folk Dance Club: *http://web.mit.edu/fdc/www*

Lion Dance Group: *http://web.mit.edu/lion-dance/www*

Movements in Time Dance Co.: *http://web.mit.edu /movements/www*

Tech Squares: *http://web.mit.edu/tech-squares/www*

Fine Arts and Crafts

Artists Behind the Desk: *http://web.mit.edu/abd*

Glass Lab: *http://web.mit.edu/glasslab*

Hobby Shop: *web.mit.edu/campus-activities/hobbyshop*

Student Art Association: *http://web.mit.edu/dsa_0002/www*

Tech Community Crafters: *http://web.http://web.mit.edu /committees*

Media

Journal Club: *http://journalclub.mit.edu/down.html*

Media In Transition: *http://web.mit.edu/sgs/www*

Rune: *http://web.mit.edu/rune/www*

Tech Gallery, The: *http://the-tech.mit.edu/Gallery*

Tech, The: *http://www-tech.mit.edu*

Technique (yearbook): *http://web.mit.edu/yearbook*

The MIT Student Cable Group: *http://mitv.mit.edu*

Thistle, The: *http://web.mit.edu/thistle/www*

Voo Doo Magazine: *http://web.mit.edu/voodoo/www /voodoo.html*

WMBR 88.1 FM: *http://wmbr.mit.edu*

Military

Air Force ROTC: *http://web.mit.edu/afrotc*

Army ROTC: *http://web.mit.edu/armyrotc*

Navy ROTC: *http://navyrotc.mit.edu*

Pershing Rifles: *http://web.mit.edu/c12abn/www*

Miscellaneous

Anime Club: *http://web.mit.edu/anime/www*

Easy Rider: The MIT Motorcycle Club: *http://web.mit.edu/ easyrider*

International Film Club: *http://web.mit.edu/ifilm/www* /Juggling Club: *http://world.std.com/·juggler*

MIT Songwriting Club: *http://web.mit.edu/songwriting/www*

MIT Vegetarian Group: *http://web.mit.edu/vsg/www*

MIT Western Hemisphere Project: *http://web.mit.edu /hemisphere/*

Science Engineering and Business Club: *http://web.mit.edu /sebc*

Science Fiction Society (MITSFS): *http://web.mit.edu /mitsfs/www*

Share a Vital Earth (SAVE): *http://web.mit.edu/save*

Societo por Esperanto: *http://web.mit.edu/esperanto/www*

Stop Our Silence (SOS): *http://web.mit.edu/stop/www*

The Society for Creative Anachronism: *http://web.mit.edu /sca/www*

Music

Chorallaries: *http://web.mit.edu/choral/www*

Concert Band: *http://web.mit.edu/bavicchi/www*

Crossproducts: *http://web.mit.edu/crossp*

Guild of Bellringers: *http://web.mit.edu/bellringers/www*

Logarhythms: *www.mitlogs.com*

Marching Band: *http://web.mit.edu/marching-band/www*

MIT Chamber Chorus: *http://web.mit.edu/mta/www/music*

MIT Chamber Music Society: *http://web.mit.edu/mta /www/music*

MIT Chamber Orchestra: *http://web.mit.edu/mta/www/music*

MIT Concert Choir: *http://web.mit.edu/mta/www/music*

MIT Festival Jazz Ensemble: *http://web.mit.edu/mta /www/music*

MIT Gamelan Galak Tika: *http://web.mit.edu/mta/www/music/*

MIT Gospel Choir: *http://web.mit.edu/mitgoscho/www*

MIT Handbell Ensemble: *http://web.mit.edu/handbell/www*

MIT Heritage of the Arts of South Asia: *http://web.mit.edu/ mta/mithas*

MIT Symphony Orchestra: *http://web.mit.edu/mta/www/music*

MIT Wind Ensemble: *http://web.mit.edu/mta/www/music*

MIT/Wellesley Toons: *http://web.mit.edu/toons/www /home.html*

Muses: *http://web.mit.edu/muses/www/welcome.html*

Music and Theater Arts: *http://web.mit.edu/mta/www*

Resonance of MIT: *http://web.mit.edu/resonance/www*

Tech Jazz Singers: *http://web.mit.edu/tjs/www*

Techiya: *http://web.mit.edu/techiya/www*

Political

College Democrats: *http://web.mit.edu/mit-cds*

College Republicans: *http://web.mit.edu/republicans/www*

Committee on Community: *http://web.mit.edu/community*

Libertarians: *http://web.mit.edu/libertarians/www*

MIT Greens: *http://web.mit.edu/greens*

MIT Objectivist Club: *http://web.mit.edu/objectivism/www/*

MIT Students for Israel: *http://web.mit.edu/mitsi/www*

Pro-Choice: *http://web.mit.edu/pro-choice/www*

Pro-Life: *http://web.mit.edu/Pro-Life/www*

Student Association for Freedom of Expression:
http://web.mit.edu/safe/www

Religious

Asian Baptist Student Koinonia: *http://web.mit.edu/absk/www*

Asian Christian Fellowship: *http://web.mit.edu/mitacf
/www/index.shtml*

Atheists, Agnostics and Humanists: *http://web.mit.edu
/mitaah/www*

Bahá'í Association: *http://web.mit.edu/mitba/www*

Baptist Student Fellowship: *http://web.mit.edu/bcm/www*

Black Christian Fellowship: *http://web.mit.edu/bcf/www*

Buddhist Association: *http://web.mit.edu/metta/www
/home.html*

Campus Crusade for Christ: *http://web.mit.edu/mitccc*

Chi Alpha Christian Fellowship: *http://web.mit.edu/xa/www*

Chinese Bible Fellowship: *http://web.mit.edu/mitcbf/www*

Chinese Christian Fellowship: *http://web.mit.edu/mitccf/www*

Christian Science Organization: *http://web.mit.edu/cso
/wwwcso.html*

Christian Student Association: *http://web.mit.edu/csa/www*

Graduate Christian Fellowship: *http://web.mit.edu/mitgcf/
www/index.shtml*

Hillel: *http://web.mit.edu/hillel/www*

Hindu Students Council: *http://web.mit.edu/hsc/www*

(Religious continued)

Hong Kong Student Bible Study Group: *http://web.mit.edu/hks-bs/www*

Lutheran-Episcopal Ministry: *http://web.mit.edu/lem*

MIT Gospel Choir: *http://web.mit.edu/mitgoscho/www*

Muslim Students' Association: *http://web.mit.edu/mitmsa/www*

Orthodox Christian Fellowship: *http://web.mit.edu/ocf/www*

Pagan Student Group: *http://web.mit.edu/psg/www*

Protestant Student Community: *http://web.mit.edu/psc/www*

Tech Catholic Community: *http://web.mit.edu/tcc/www*

United Christian Fellowship: *http://web.mit.edu/ucf/www*

United Christian R/O: *http://web.mit.edu/christro/www*

Student Government

Association of Student Activities: *http://web.mit.edu/asa/www*

Graduate Student Council: *http://web.mit.edu/gsc/www*

UA Class of 2003 Council: *http://web.mit.edu/2003*

UA Class of 2004 Council: *http://web.mit.edu/2004*

UA Class of 2005 Council: *http://web.mit.edu/2005*

UA Class of 2006 Council: *http://web.mit.edu/2006*

Undergraduate Association (UA): *http://web.mit.edu/ua/www*

Support Groups

Gay, Lesbian, and Bisexual Graduate Student Coffeehouse: *http://web.mit.edu/glb-coffee/www*

Gays, Lesbians, and Bisexuals at MIT (GAMIT): *http://web.mit.edu/gamit/www*

Lesbian, Bisexual, Gay, and Transgendered at MIT: *http://web.mit.edu/lbgt*

Queer Women Looking for Life in Tech School: *http://web.mit.edu/qwillts*

Sloan LGBT: *http://web.mit.edu/lgbt/sloan*

Stop Our Silence (SOS): *http://web.mit.edu/stop/www*

Theatre

Black Theatre Guild: *http://web.mit.edu/blacktg/www/home.html*

Community Players: *http://web.mit.edu/mitcp/www*

Dramashop: *http://web.mit.edu/dramashop/www*

Gilbert & Sullivan Players: *http://web.mit.edu/gsp/www*

Music & Theater Arts Recognized Activities: *http://web.mit.edu/mta/www/music*

Musical Theatre Guild: *http://web.mit.edu/mtg/www*

Shakespeare Ensemble: *http://web.mit.edu/ensemble/www*

Women's Groups

Association of MIT Alumnae (AMITA): *http://www.mit-amita.org*

Black Women's Alliance: *http://web.mit.edu/black-women/www*

Family Resource Center: *http://web.mit.edu/hr/worklife*

Graduate Student Women: *http://web.mit.edu/gso*

Graduate Women of Course 6 (EECS): *http://web.mit.edu/gw6/www*

McCormick Hall: http://web.mit.edu/mccormick/www

Muses: *http://web.mit.edu/mccormick/www*

Society of Women Engineers (SWE): *http://web.mit.edu/swe/www*

SOS: Significant Others of Sloan (Wives' Group): *http://web.mit.edu/sos*

spouses&partners@mit: *http://web.mit.edu/medical/spousesandpartners*

Women in Physics: *http://web.mit.edu/physics/wphys*

Women's Forum: *http://web.mit.edu/committees/womensforum*

Women's Independent Living Group (WILG): *http://web.mit.edu/wilg/www*

Women's League (WL): *http://web.mit.edu/womensleague*

Women's Studies: *http://web.mit.edu/womens-studies/www*

Women's Technology Program: *http://wtp.mit.edu*

The Best
& Worst

The Ten **BEST** Things About MIT

1	Outstanding professors
2	Student-faculty research opportunities
3	Athena
4	The truly wonderful student body
5	The city of Boston and all its resources
6	Killian Kickoff
7	Fabulous museums
8	A safe and secure campus
9	The Pour House
10	An abundance of Greek organizations to choose from

The Ten WORST Things About MIT

1 GIRs

2 The intense workload

3 Not enough hot, single women on campus

4 Bland campus food

5 Realizing that you might not be the smartest anymore

6 Campus police busting up frat parties

7 Students who think they're better than others

8 Student apathy toward varsity sports

9 Strict alcohol policies

10 Getting over the whole MIT stigma

Visiting

The Lowdown On...
Visiting

Hotel Information:

A Cambridge House Bed & Breakfast Inn

www.acambridgehouse.com
2218 Massachusetts Avenue
Cambridge, MA 02140
(617) 491-6300
Distance From Campus:
4 miles
Price Range: $109–$290

Boston Marriott Cambridge

www.marriott.com
2 Cambridge Center
Broadway & Third Streets
Cambridge, MA 02142
(617) 494-6600
Distance From Campus:
About 1 mile
Price Range: $199–$289

Cambridge Gateway Inn

www.cambridgegatewayinn.com

211 Concord Turnpike
Route 2 East
Cambridge, MA 02140
(617) 661-7800
Distance From Campus:
5 miles
Price Range: $90–$127

The Charles Hotel at Harvard Square

www.charleshotel.com

One Bennett Street
Cambridge, MA 02138
(617) 864-1200
Distance From Campus:
2 miles
Price Range: $230–$400

The Eliot Hotel

www.eliothotel.com

370 Commonwealth Avenue
Boston, MA 02215
(617) 267-1607
Distance from Campus:
1 mile
Price Range: $195–$235

Harding House

www.irvinghouse.com

288 Harvard Street
Cambridge, MA 02139
(617) 876-2888
Distance From Campus:
1 mile
Price Range: $60–$100

Hilton/Logan Airport

www.loganairport.com

85 Terminal Road
Boston, MA 02128
(617) 568-6700
Distance From Campus:
6 miles
Price Range: $120–$199

Holiday Inn Select at Government Center

www.holiday-inn.com

5 Blossom Street
Boston, MA 02114
(617) 742-7630
Distance From Campus:
2 miles
Price Range: $155–$230

Hyatt Regency Cambridge

www.cambridge.hyatt.com

575 Memorial Drive
Cambridge, MA 02139
(617) 492-1234
Distance from Campus: 1 mile
Price Range: $179 and up

Irving House

www.irvinghouse.com

24 Irving Street
Cambridge, MA 02138
(617) 547-4600
Distance From Campus:
2 miles
Price Range: $85–$165

The Kendall Hotel

www.kendallhotel.com

350 Main Street

Cambridge, MA 02142

(617) 577-1300

Distance From Campus:
About 1 mile

Price Range: $149 - $229

Radisson Hotel Cambridge

*www.radisson.com/
cambridgema*

777 Memorial Drive

Cambridge, MA 02139

(617) 492-7777

Distance From Campus:
2 miles

Price Range: $159 - $199

Royal Sonesta Hotel

www.royalsonestaboston.com

5 Cambridge Parkway

Cambridge, MA 02142

(617) 806-4200

Distance From Campus:
2 miles

Price Range: $239 - $450

Sheraton Commander Hotel

www.sheratoncommander.com

16 Garden Street

Cambridge, MA 02138

Phone: (617) 547-4800

Distance From Campus:
3 miles

Price Range: $245 - $365

University Park Hotel

www.hotelatmit.com

20 Sidney Street

Cambridge, MA 02139

(617) 577-0200

Distance From Campus:
About 1 mile

Price Range: $139 to $259

Take a Campus Virtual Tour

http://web.mit.edu/vrtour

Group Information Session or Interview

Information sessions are offered Monday through Friday at
10 a.m. and 2 p.m. at the following address:

Admissions Reception Center
77 Massachusetts Avenue
Building 10, Room 100

Campus Tours

Campus tours are Monday through Friday at 10:45 a.m. and
2:45 p.m. starting at 77 Massachusetts Avenue, Lobby 7. These
tours are student led and are held immediately following
information sessions.

If your group is larger than 15, please call the Information
Center at (617) 253-1875 at least two weeks in advance.
Otherwise, no reservations are necessary.

Overnight Visits

Any high school senior or junior is welcome to stay overnight
during the fall term. However, in the spring term, MIT would
prefer overnight visits to be limited only to students who have
already been admitted. Overnight housing is arranged on any
Sunday through Friday evenings, except during MIT or public
holidays and exam periods. There is no charge for housing.

For more information, check: *http://web.mit.edu/admissions/
www/undergrad/visiting/index.html*

Directions to Campus

Driving from the North

From South I-93
- Take the exit for MA-3.
- Continue on MA-3, it will become MA-3/MA-28.
- Continue on MA-3, going over the Longfellow Bridge.
- MA-3 will turn into Main Street.
- Turn right on Memorial Drive.
- Turn right on Massachusetts Avenue and follow it for about a half mile.

From South I-95
- Take the I-93 South Exit
- Take the exit for MA-3.
- Continue on MA-3, it will become MA-3/MA-28.
- Continue on MA-3, going over the Longfellow Bridge.
- MA-3 will turn into Main Street.
- Turn right on Memorial Drive.
- Turn right on Massachusetts Avenue.
- The main entrance to MIT will be on your left.

Driving from the South

From North I-93
- Follow I-93 (The Southeast Expressway) into Boston.
- Take the exit for MA-3.
- Continue on MA-3, it will become MA-3/MA-28.
- Continue on MA-3, going over the Longfellow Bridge.
- MA-3 will turn into Main Street.
- Turn right on Memorial Drive.
- Turn right on Massachusetts Avenue.
- The entrance will be on the left.

From North I-95
- Take the I-93 North exit
- Take the exit for MA-3.
- Continue on MA-3, it will become MA-3/MA-28.
- Continue on MA-3, going over the Longfellow Bridge.
- MA-3 will turn into Main Street.
- Turn right on Memorial Drive.
- Turn right on Massachusetts Avenue and follow it for about a half mile.

Driving from the West

From East I-90

- Take the Cambridge/Brighton exit (exit 18).
- Following the signs to Cambridge, cross the River Street Bridge.
- Continue going straight about 1 mile to Central Square.
- Turn right on Massachusetts Avenue and follow it for about a half mile to the entrance.

Driving from the Airport

Starting from ACCESS RD

- Bear right to take MA-1A
- Take the I-93 NORTH exit.
- Take the exit for MA-3.
- Continue on MA-3, it will become MA-3/MA-28.
- Continue on MA-3, going over the Longfellow Bridge.
- MA-3 will turn into Main Street.
- Turn right on Memorial Drive.
- Turn right on Massachusetts Avenue.
- The entrance will be on your left.

Words to Know

Academic Probation – A suspension imposed on a student if he or she fails to keep up with the school's minimum academic requirements. Those unable to improve their grades after receiving this warning can face dismissal.

Beer Pong/Beirut – A drinking game involving cups of beer arranged in a pyramid shape on each side of a table. The goal is to get a ping pong ball into one of the opponent's cups by throwing the ball or hitting it with a paddle. If the ball lands in a cup, the opponent is required to drink the beer.

Bid – An invitation from a fraternity or sorority to 'pledge' (join) that specific house.

Blue-Light Phone – Brightly-colored phone posts with a blue light bulb on top. These phones exist for security purposes and are located at various outside locations around most campuses. In an emergency, a student can pick up one of these phones (free of charge) to connect with campus police or a security escort.

Campus Police – Police who are specifically assigned to a given institution. Campus police are typically not regular city officers; they are employed by the university in a full-time capacity.

Club Sports – A level of sports that falls somewhere between varsity and intramural. If a student is unable to commit to a varsity team but has a lot of passion for athletics, a club sport could be a better, less intense option. Even less demanding, intramural (IM) sports often involve no traveling and considerably less time.

Cocaine – An illegal drug. Also known as "coke" or "blow," cocaine often resembles a white crystalline or powdery substance. It is highly addictive and dangerous.

Common Application – An application with which students can apply to multiple schools.

Course Registration – The period of official class selection for the upcoming quarter or semester. Prior to registration, it is best to prepare several back-up courses in case a particular class becomes full. If a course is full, students can place themselves on the waitlist, although this still does not guarantee entry.

Division Athletics – Athletic classifications range from Division I to Division III. Division IA is the most competitive, while Division III is considered to be the least competitive.

Dorm – A dorm (or dormitory) is an on-campus housing facility. Dorms can provide a range of options from suite-style rooms to more communal options that include shared bathrooms. Most first-year students live in dorms. Some upperclassmen who wish to stay on campus also choose this option.

Early Action – An application option with which a student can apply to a school and receive an early acceptance response without a binding commitment. This system is becoming less and less available.

Early Decision – An application option that students should use only if they are certain they plan to attend the school in question. If a student applies using the early decision option and is admitted, he or she is required and bound to attend that university. Admission rates are usually higher among students who apply through early decision, as the student is clearly indicating that the school is his or her first choice.

Ecstasy – An illegal drug. Also known as "E" or "X," ecstasy looks like a pill and most resembles an aspirin. Considered a party drug, ecstasy is very dangerous and can be deadly.

Ethernet – An extremely fast Internet connection available in most university-owned residence halls. To use an Ethernet connection properly, a student will need a network card and cable for his or her computer.

Fake ID – A counterfeit identification card that contains false information. Most commonly, students get fake IDs with altered birthdates so that they appear to be older than 21 (and therefore of legal drinking age). Even though it is illegal, many college students have fake IDs in hopes of purchasing alcohol or getting into bars.

Frosh – Slang for "freshman" or "freshmen."

Hazing – Initiation rituals administered by some fraternities or sororities as part of the pledging process. Many universities have outlawed hazing due to its degrading, and sometimes dangerous, nature.

Intramurals (IMs) – A popular, and usually free, sport league in which students create teams and compete against one another. These sports vary in competitiveness and can include a range of activities—everything from billiards to water polo. IM sports are a great way to meet people with similar interests.

Keg – Officially called a half-barrel, a keg contains roughly 200 12-ounce servings of beer.

LSD – An illegal drug, also known as acid, this hallucinogenic drug most commonly resembles a tab of paper.

Marijuana – An illegal drug, also known as weed or pot; along with alcohol, marijuana is one of the most commonly-found drugs on campuses across the country.

Major –The focal point of a student's college studies; a specific topic that is studied for a degree. Examples of majors include physics, English, history, computer science, economics, business, and music. Many students decide on a specific major before arriving on campus, while others are simply "undecided" until declaring a major. Those who are extremely interested in two areas can also choose to double major.

Meal Block – The equivalent of one meal. Students on a meal plan usually receive a fixed number of meals per week. Each meal, or "block," can be redeemed at the school's dining facilities in place of cash. Often, a student's weekly allotment of meal blocks will be forfeited if not used.

Minor – An additional focal point in a student's education. Often serving as a complement or addition to a student's main area of focus, a minor has fewer requirements and prerequisites to fulfill than a major. Minors are not required for graduation from most schools; however some students who want to explore many different interests choose to pursue both a major and a minor.

Mushrooms – An illegal drug. Also known as "'shrooms," this drug resembles regular mushrooms but is extremely hallucinogenic.

Off-Campus Housing – Housing from a particular landlord or rental group that is not affiliated with the university. Depending on the college, off-campus housing can range from extremely popular to non-existent. Students who choose to live off campus are typically given more freedom, but they also have to deal with possible subletting scenarios, furniture, bills, and other issues. In addition to these factors, rental prices and distance often affect a student's decision to move off campus.

Office Hours – Time that teachers set aside for students who have questions about coursework. Office hours are a good forum for students to go over any problems and to show interest in the subject material.

Pledging – The early phase of joining a fraternity or sorority, pledging takes place after a student has gone through rush and received a bid. Pledging usually lasts between one and two semesters. Once the pledging period is complete and a particular student has done everything that is required to become a member, that student is considered a brother or sister. If a fraternity or a sorority would decide to "haze" a group of students, this initiation would take place during the pledging period.

Private Institution – A school that does not use tax revenue to subsidize education costs. Private schools typically cost more than public schools and are usually smaller.

Prof – Slang for "professor."

Public Institution – A school that uses tax revenue to subsidize education costs. Public schools are often a good value for in-state residents and tend to be larger than most private colleges.

Quarter System (or Trimester System) – A type of academic calendar system. In this setup, students take classes for three academic periods. The first quarter usually starts in late September or early October and concludes right before Christmas. The second quarter usually starts around early to mid–January and finishes up around March or April. The last academic quarter, or "third quarter," usually starts in late March or early April and finishes up in late May or Mid-June. The fourth quarter is summer. The major difference between the quarter system and semester system is that students take more, less comprehensive courses under the quarter calendar.

RA (Resident Assistant) – A student leader who is assigned to a particular floor in a dormitory in order to help to the other students who live there. An RA's duties include ensuring student safety and providing assistance wherever possible.

Recitation – An extension of a specific course; a review session. Some classes, particularly large lectures, are supplemented with mandatory recitation sessions that provide a relatively personal class setting.

Rolling Admissions – A form of admissions. Most commonly found at public institutions, schools with this type of policy continue to accept students throughout the year until their class sizes are met. For example, some schools begin accepting students as early as December and will continue to do so until April or May.

Room and Board – This figure is typically the combined cost of a university-owned room and a meal plan.

Room Draw/Housing Lottery – A common way to pick on-campus room assignments for the following year. If a student decides to remain in university-owned housing, he or she is assigned a unique number that, along with seniority, is used to determine his or her housing for the next year.

Rush – The period in which students can meet the brothers and sisters of a particular chapter and find out if a given fraternity or sorority is right for them. Rushing a fraternity or a sorority is not a requirement at any school. The goal of rush is to give students who are serious about pledging a feel for what to expect.

Semester System – The most common type of academic calendar system at college campuses. This setup typically includes two semesters in a given school year. The fall semester starts around the end of August or early September and concludes before winter vacation. The spring semester usually starts in mid-January and ends in late April or May.

Student Center/Rec Center/Student Union – A common area on campus that often contains study areas, recreation facilities, and eateries. This building is often a good place to meet up with fellow students; depending on the school, the student center can have a huge role or a non-existent role in campus life.

Student ID – A university-issued photo ID that serves as a student's key to school-related functions. Some schools require students to show these cards in order to get into dorms, libraries, cafeterias, and other facilities. In addition to storing meal plan information, in some cases, a student ID can actually work as a debit card and allow students to purchase things from bookstores or local shops.

Suite – A type of dorm room. Unlike dorms that feature communal bathrooms shared by the entire floor, suites offer bathrooms shared only among the suite. Suite-style dorm rooms can house anywhere from two to ten students.

TA (Teacher's Assistant) – An undergraduate or grad student who helps in some manner with a specific course. In some cases, a TA will teach a class, assist a professor, grade assignments, or conduct office hours.

Undergraduate – A student in the process of studying for his or her bachelor's degree.

ABOUT THE AUTHOR

My name is Susie Lee, and I'm a rising junior at MIT. It's funny that I wrote this because I actually didn't want to go to MIT when I was a high school senior; I never would have bought a book like this because I just didn't care about it. In fact, I only applied because I was already applying to a dozen other schools (what was one more?). But, plans change, and three years later here I am, and I am thankful every day for my decision. My major is management, and my double major and/or minor(s) changes every day. Other than that, I am active in my sorority, my research job, and the campus, in general.

I am originally from Granger, Indiana, a small town near South Bend. And being from the Midwest, I had no idea what to expect from Boston or MIT. As I read everything that I have written, I realized that I knew almost none of the things about MIT included in this book when I first applied here. Writing this book has caused me to re-examine my entire MIT experience at the exact time when I was starting to take everything for granted.

Aside from all this generic info, some of my favorite things include: good food, good books, Disney World, math, card games, Notre Dame college football, sleeping, and beautiful sunny weather.

There is a long list of people whom I would like to thank. The most important people are my family. I am working as hard as I can in this life to make all the work my parents have done worthwhile. They are always proud and supportive of me in every way. Even if my picture doesn't end up on this page, I know my dad will buy 10 copies anyway. I also want to thank my sister, Cecile, for teaching me about the things that really matter in life, and for always making me smile.

Other than that, I want to thank the following people: Dave for helping me understand who I am, Christy for being the only one to reply to my ridiculous e-mail, Kathryn for giving long, useful answers, Val for all of her help, Michelle for being a great roommate, and all the people at College Prowler for giving me this chance.

E-mail me at susielee@collegeprowler.com! Thanks again!

The College Prowler Big Book of Colleges

Having Trouble Narrowing Down Your Choices?
Try Going Bigger!

BIG BOOK OF COLLEGES '09
7¼" X 10", 1248 Pages Paperback
$29.95 Retail
978-1-4274-0005-5

Choosing the perfect school can be an overwhelming challenge. Luckily, our *Big Book of Colleges* makes that task a little less daunting. We've packed it with overviews of our full library of single-school guides—more than 280 of the nation's top schools—giving you some much-needed perspective on your search.

College Prowler on the Web

Craving some electronic interaction? Check out the new and improved **CollegeProwler.com**! We've included the COMPLETE contents of more than 250 of our single-school guides on the Web—and you can gain access to all of them for just $39.95 per year!

Not only that, but non-subscribers can still view and compare our grades for each school, order books at our online bookstore, or enter our monthly scholarship contest. Don't get left in the dark when making your college decision. Let College Prowler be your guide!

Get the Jolt!

College Jolt gives you a peek behind the scenes

College Jolt is our new blog designed to hook you up with great information, funny videos, cool contests, awesome scholarship opportunities, and honest insight into who we are and what we're all about.

Check us out at ***www.collegejolt.com***

Tell Us What Life Is Really Like at Your School!

Have you ever wanted to let people know what your college is really like? Now's your chance to help millions of high school students choose the right college.

Let your voice be heard.

Check out *www.collegeprowler.com* for more info!

Need More Help?

Do you have more questions about this school? Can't find a certain statistic? College Prowler is here to help. We are the best source of college information out there. We have a network of thousands of students who can get the latest information on any school to you ASAP. E-mail us at info@collegeprowler.com with your college-related questions.

E-Mail Us Your College-Related Questions!

Check out *www.collegeprowler.com* for more details.
1-800-290-2682

Write For Us!
Get published! Voice your opinion.

Writing a College Prowler guidebook is both fun and rewarding; our open-ended format allows your own creativity free reign. Our writers have been featured in national newspapers and have seen their names in bookstores across the country. Now is your chance to break into the publishing industry with one of the country's fastest-growing publishers!

Apply now at ***www.collegeprowler.com***

Contact editor@collegeprowler.com or call 1-800-290-2682 for more details.

Pros and Cons

Still can't figure out if this is the right school for you?
You've already read through this in-depth guide;
why not list the pros and cons? It will really help
with narrowing down your decision and determining
whether or not this school is right for you.

Pros	Cons
....	....
....	....
....	....
....	....
....	....
....	....
....	....
....	....
....	....
....	....
....	....
....	....
....	....

Pros and Cons

Still can't figure out if this is the right school for you?
You've already read through this in-depth guide;
why not list the pros and cons? It will really help
with narrowing down your decision and determining
whether or not this school is right for you.

Pros	Cons
....	....
....	....
....	....
....	....
....	....
....	....
....	....
....	....
....	....
....	....
....	....
....	....
....	....

Notes

....

....

....

....

....

....

....

....

....

....

....

....

....

Notes

....

....

....

....

....

....

....

....

....

....

....

....

....

Notes

....

....

....

....

....

....

....

....

....

....

....

....

....

Notes

....

....

....

....

....

....

....

....

....

....

....

....

....

Notes

Notes

....

....

....

....

....

....

....

....

....

....

....

....

....

Notes

Notes

....

....

....

....

....

....

....

....

....

....

....

....

....

Notes

....

....

....

....

....

....

....

....

....

....

....

....

....

Notes

....

....

....

....

....

....

....

....

....

....

....

....

....

Notes

....

....

....

....

....

....

....

....

....

....

....

....

....

....

Notes

....

....

....

....

....

....

....

....

....

....

....

....

....

Notes

....

....

....

....

....

....

....

....

....

....

....

....

....

Notes

....

....

....

....

....

....

....

....

....

....

....

....

....

Notes

....

....

....

....

....

....

....

....

....

....

....

....

....

Notes

....

....

....

....

....

....

....

....

....

....

....

....

....

Notes

Notes

....

....

....

....

....

....

....

....

....

....

....

....

....

Notes

....

....

....

....

....

....

....

....

....

....

....

....

....

Notes

....

....

....

....

....

....

....

....

....

....

....

....

....

Notes

....

....

....

....

....

....

....

....

....

....

....

....

....

Notes

....

....

....

....

....

....

....

....

....

....

....

....

....

Notes

....
....
....
....
....
....
....
....
....
....
....
....
....

Notes

....

....

....

....

....

....

....

....

....

....

....

....

....

Notes

....

....

....

....

....

....

....

....

....

....

....

....

....

Notes

....

....

....

....

....

....

....

....

....

....

....

....

....

Notes

....

....

....

....

....

....

....

....

....

....

....

....

....

Notes

....

....

....

....

f

....

....

....

....

....

....

....

....

....

Albion College
Alfred University
Allegheny College
American University
Amherst College
Arizona State University
Auburn University
Babson College
Ball State University
Bard College
Barnard College
Bates College
Baylor University
Beloit College
Bentley College
Binghamton University
Birmingham Southern College
Boston College
Boston University
Bowdoin College
Brandeis University
Brigham Young University
Brown University
Bryn Mawr College
Bucknell University
Cal Poly
Cal Poly Pomona
Cal State Northridge
Cal State Sacramento
Caltech
Carleton College
Carnegie Mellon University
Case Western Reserve
Centenary College of Louisiana
Centre College
Claremont McKenna College
Clark Atlanta University
Clark University
Clemson University
Colby College
Colgate University
College of Charleston
College of the Holy Cross
College of William & Mary
College of Wooster
Colorado College
Columbia University
Connecticut College
Cornell University
Creighton University
CUNY Hunters College
Dartmouth College
Davidson College
Denison University
DePauw University
Dickinson College
Drexel University
Duke University
Duquesne University
Earlham College
East Carolina University
Elon University
Emerson College
Emory University
FIT
Florida State University
Fordham University

Franklin & Marshall College
Furman University
Geneva College
George Washington University
Georgetown University
Georgia Tech
Gettysburg College
Gonzaga University
Goucher College
Grinnell College
Grove City College
Guilford College
Gustavus Adolphus College
Hamilton College
Hampshire College
Hampton University
Hanover College
Harvard University
Harvey Mudd College
Haverford College
Hofstra University
Hollins University
Howard University
Idaho State University
Illinois State University
Illinois Wesleyan University
Indiana University
Iowa State University
Ithaca College
IUPUI
James Madison University
Johns Hopkins University
Juniata College
Kansas State
Kent State University
Kenyon College
Lafayette College
LaRoche College
Lawrence University
Lehigh University
Lewis & Clark College
Louisiana State University
Loyola College in Maryland
Loyola Marymount University
Loyola University Chicago
Loyola University New Orleans
Macalester College
Marlboro College
Marquette University
McGill University
Miami University of Ohio
Michigan State University
Middle Tennessee State
Middlebury College
Millsaps College
MIT
Montana State University
Mount Holyoke College
Muhlenberg College
New York University
North Carolina State
Northeastern University
Northern Arizona University
Northern Illinois University
Northwestern University
Oberlin College
Occidental College

Ohio State University
Ohio University
Ohio Wesleyan University
Old Dominion University
Penn State University
Pepperdine University
Pitzer College
Pomona College
Princeton University
Providence College
Purdue University
Reed College
Rensselaer Polytechnic Institute
Rhode Island School of Design
Rhodes College
Rice University
Rochester Institute of Technology
Rollins College
Rutgers University
San Diego State University
Santa Clara University
Sarah Lawrence College
Scripps College
Seattle University
Seton Hall University
Simmons College
Skidmore College
Slippery Rock
Smith College
Southern Methodist University
Southwestern University
Spelman College
St. Joseph's University Philadelphia
St. John's University
St. Louis University
St. Olaf College
Stanford University
Stetson University
Stony Brook University
Susquanna University
Swarthmore College
Syracuse University
Temple University
Tennessee State University
Texas A & M University
Texas Christian University
Towson University
Trinity College Connecticut
Trinity University Texas
Truman State
Tufts University
Tulane University
UC Berkeley
UC Davis
UC Irvine
UC Riverside
UC San Diego
UC Santa Barbara
UC Santa Cruz
UCLA
Union College
University at Albany
University at Buffalo
University of Alabama
University of Arizona
University of Central Florida
University of Chicago

University of Colorado
University of Connecticut
University of Delaware
University of Denver
University of Florida
University of Georgia
University of Illinois
University of Iowa
University of Kansas
University of Kentucky
University of Maine
University of Maryland
University of Massachusetts
University of Miami
University of Michigan
University of Minnesota
University of Mississippi
University of Missouri
University of Nebraska
University of New Hampshire
University of North Carolina
University of Notre Dame
University of Oklahoma
University of Oregon
University of Pennsylvania
University of Pittsburgh
University of Puget Sound
University of Rhode Island
University of Richmond
University of Rochester
University of San Diego
University of San Francisco
University of South Carolina
University of South Dakota
University of South Florida
University of Southern California
University of Tennessee
University of Texas
University of Utah
University of Vermont
University of Virginia
University of Washington
University of Wisconsin
UNLV
Ursinus College
Valparaiso University
Vanderbilt University
Vassar College
Villanova University
Virginia Tech
Wake Forest University
Warren Wilson College
Washington and Lee University
Washington University in St. Louis
Wellesley College
Wesleyan University
West Point
West Virginia University
Wheaton College IL
Wheaton College MA
Whitman College
Wilkes University
Williams College
Xavier University
Yale University

1898226

Made in the USA